EYEWITNESS GUIDES

FUTURE

Written by
MICHAEL TAMBINI

A buckyball

DK

DORLING KINDERSLEY
London • New York •
Stuttgart • Moscow • Sydney

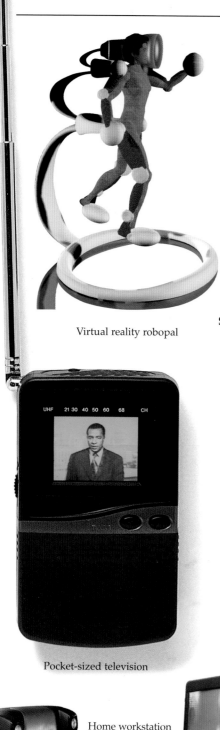

Virtual reality robopal

Pocket-sized television

Home workstation
in the year 2020

Millennium
Tower, Tokyo

A DORLING KINDERSLEY BOOK

Senior editor Miranda Smith
Editor Helena Spiteri
Senior art editor Jane Bull
Art editor Joanne Connor
Senior managing editor Linda Martin
Senior managing art editor Julia Harris
Production Lisa Moss
Picture research Sam Ruston
DTP Designer Nicky Studdart
Consultant Ian Pearson
Special photography Andy Crawford, David Exton

This Eyewitness ® Guide has been conceived by
Dorling Kindersley Limited and Editions Gallimard

First published in Great Britain in 1998
by Dorling Kindersley Limited,
9 Henrietta Street, London WC2E 8PS

A CIP catalogue record for this book is
available from the British Library.

ISBN 0 7513 61283

Colour reproduction by
Colourscan, Singapore
Printed in Singapore by Toppan

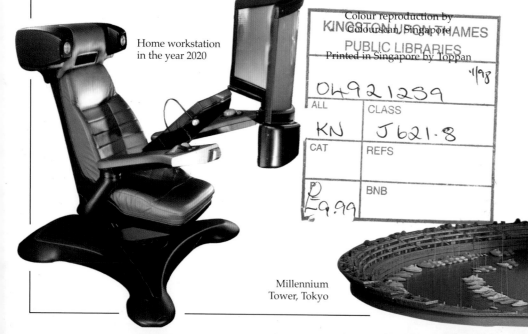

Contents

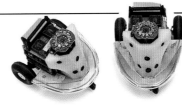

A brave new world

WE ARE FASCINATED by the future, and excited by thinking about what might happen next. Through history, many people have tried to predict the future. Fortune-tellers and prophets utter words of doom and warning, while futurologists anticipate scientific and social changes by analyzing existing trends. Imagine the 20th century without the motor car, telephones, computers, the atom bomb, space travel, and the discovery of DNA. They have all made a profound impact on us, but which of them were predicted to take place?

CRYSTAL-GAZING
For centuries, mystics and fortune-tellers have given predictions. But their utterances owed more to a knowledge of human nature than anything else.

Different lines represent different characteristics

PALM READING
A popular form of prophesy is palm reading, which originated in India and has been practised for hundreds of years. It is believed that a person's character and future can be discovered by the interpretation of the natural markings on their hands.

The Hand

NOSTRADAMUS
The prophecies of Nostradamus were first published in the 16th century and many believe he accurately foretold the future. He is said to have predicted the Great Fire of London and air battles in the 20th century.

Characters often signify future fates

READING CARDS
Cards are frequently used to predict the future. Before a reading can be made, the cards have to be shuffled, placed face down, then turned over one by one.

SCIENCE FICTION
Science fiction writers are some of the most active forecasters of the future. Writers such as Jules Verne, H. G. Wells, Arthur C. Clarke, and Isaac Asimov have depicted worlds we may know well in the future.

DELPHIC ORACLE
In Greece, at the foot of Mount Parnassus, stood the temple of Apollo. Here Apollo spoke through his priestess, who predicted the future and gave guidance. Today, the closest we have to oracles are the futurologists whose predictions are based on scientific information.

1900

I never think of the future – it comes soon enough

ALBERT EINSTEIN

ALBERT EINSTEIN
In 1905, Einstein proposed a theory of relativity, which was to revolutionize physics. He later outlined a complete theory of gravity that explained how the Universe works.

TAKING PICTURES
Black-and-white photography became very popular at the turn of the century. But when the Lumière brothers developed colour film in 1907, there was a surge of interest in photography.

Pilot lay on his stomach

Wings gently twisted to control flight

TAKING FLIGHT
In 1903, the Wright brothers flew for just 12 seconds, covering a distance of 44 m (120 ft), and scarcely anyone paid attention. Yet this event changed the world. Today, we think nothing of travelling halfway round the world by jumbo jet.

INVENTIONS
1901 First transatlantic radio broadcast
1901 Hubert Cecil Booth manufactures the first vacuum cleaner
1903 Wright brothers make first powered flight
1907 Lumière brothers develop colour photography
1907 French bicycle-maker Paul Cornu's motor-driven helicopter takes to the air

EVENTS
1900 Sigmund Freud publishes his book *The Interpretation of Dreams*
1902 Boer War ends in South Africa
1904 Japanese attack Port Arthur at start of Russo-Japanese War
1905 Albert Einstein proposes his theory of relativity
1908 Two-year-old Pu Yi ascends throne of China

1910

Time present and time past are both perhaps present in time future, and time future contained in time past

T. S. ELIOT

MAKING CONTACT
The invention of the telephone began the great communications revolution. For the first time, it was possible to talk directly to people over great distances.

METAL THAT LASTS
By adding chromium to steel in 1913, it was found that the new metal would not rust or scratch. Stainless steel has become a popular part of everyday life.

EASY TRANSPORT
Henry Ford was the first person to mass-produce the car, changing the nature of factory work, as well as giving us the freedom to travel.

1913 Mass production of Ford's Model T begins
1913 Stainless steel first cast in Sheffield, UK
1914 First traffic lights introduced in Cleveland, Ohio, in the US
1915 Heat-resistant glass Pyrex marketed
1915 First transcontinental telephone call between New York and San Francisco
1916 First tank goes into battle

1911 Norwegian Roald Amundsen reaches the South Pole
1911 Revolution in China overthrows the Ch'ing dynasty
1912 *Titanic* sinks in the Atlantic
1914 Start of World War I, which ends with German surrender in 1918
1917 Tsar Nicholas II overthrown in Russia

1920

The most distressing thing that can happen to a prophet is to be proved wrong. The next most distressing thing is to be proved right

ALDOUS HUXLEY

A SCREEN IN THE LIVING-ROOM
For more than half a century, television has provided us with news, drama, and documentaries. Viewers in the home have been eyewitnesses to historic events from civil wars to the death of a president.

WALL STREET CRASH
The Wall Street stock market crash in 1929 led to financial crisis across the world. In the United States, farming businesses collapsed, unemployment rose, and banks failed.

1920 "Tommy" sub-machine gun patented
1921 18 million Russians starve because of severe drought
1921 First motorway opens in Germany
1922 Canadian becomes first diabetic to be treated with insulin
1926 John Logie Baird transmits first television pictures

1920 Prohibition comes into force in US
1922 Tutankhamun's tomb uncovered, Egypt
1928 Flying doctor service begins in Australia
1928 Scottish bacteriologist Alexander Fleming discovers penicillin
1929 US Wall Street Crash leads to world financial crisis

1930

You cannot fight against the future. Time is on our side

WILLIAM GLADSTONE

Nylon stockings

NYLON
Few materials have had such an impact on the fashion industry as nylon. This manufactured material was used to make many different products.

Whittle's jet engine

JET ENGINE
In 1937, UK scientist Frank Whittle built the first prototype of a jet engine, which was put to practical use in 1941. Today, jet aircraft can travel faster than the speed of sound.

WRITING OF THE FUTURE
H. G. Wells wrote many science fiction novels, including *The War of the Worlds* in which the Earth is invaded.

Wells at work on a novel

1930 Nylon developed by Wallace Carothers
1933 German post office opens first "telex" service between Berlin and Hamburg
1934 UK inventor Percy Shaw patents cat's-eye road studs
1937 Engineer Frank Whittle builds prototype of the first jet engine
1939 First washing machine exhibited in UK

1930 US Clyde Tombaugh discovers Pluto
1936 Spanish Civil War begins
1937 Airship *Hindenburg* bursts into flames killing 35 of the 97 on board
1938 Orson Welles broadcasts convincing radio version of H. G. Wells' *War of the Worlds*
1939 Germany, under Adolph Hitler, invades Poland and starts World War II

Continued on next page

1940

We have to live with the bugs and the bomb not for the next ten years but the next ten thousand

ARTHUR KOESTLER

Distinctive mushroom cloud

ATOM BOMB
The atom bombs that destroyed Hiroshima and Nagasaki in 1945 left few doubts about their awesome potential and so began an arms race between world powers.

ARTHUR C. CLARKE
Arthur C. Clarke has written many science fiction novels about space exploration. He also predicted the use of satellites for global communications.

1950

We are going to have to be rather clever to escape from our own cleverness in the past

SIR MARK OLIPHANT

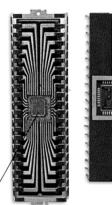

DINERS' CLUB
The Diners' Club card was set up to make it easier for executives to eat out on a company account. Now credit cards are used by most people all over the world.

SILICON CHIP
The impact of silicon chips on this century cannot be overstated. Tiny wafers of silicon carry thousands of electrical components and feature in everything from computers to cars.

Silicon chip

CRICK AND WATSON
In 1953, Frances Crick and James Watson discovered the molecular structure of DNA. The genetic code for all life is contained within this molecule. Our ability to understand and manipulate it will be central to the 21st century.

1960

TELSTAR
Telstar was the first communications satellite to orbit the Earth. It was owned by the American Telephone and Telegraph Company and launched by NASA.

The future is called perhaps, which is the only possible thing to call it. And the most important thing is not to allow it to scare you

TENNESSEE WILLIAMS

MAN ON THE MOON
As Neil Armstrong stepped onto the Moon he uttered the now historic words, "That's one small step for man, one giant leap for mankind". The exploration of Space is still in its infancy, yet humans seem driven to explore and people are certain to follow in Neil Armstrong's footsteps.

Neil Armstrong on the surface of the Moon

INVENTIONS

1941	World's first aerosol can patented in US
1943	Dutch doctor Wilhelm Kolff makes first artificial kidney machine
1945	Arthur C. Clarke predicts satellites in geostationary orbit for global communications
1945	Microwave oven patented in US
1947	First transistor made in US
1949	Maiden flight of Comet jet

1950	First credit card, Diner's Club, introduced
1951	US engineers John Eckert and John Mauchly invent digital computer UNIVAC
1957	USSR launches Sputnik 1, first artificial satellite in space
1959	UK designer Christopher Cockerell invents the hovercraft
1959	First silicon chip manufactured

1960	Theodore Maiman builds the laser
1962	First communications satellite, Telstar I, put into orbit.
1963	Tape cassette machine patented by Phillips, Holland
1966	Vertical take-off and landing (VTOL) aircraft unveiled at air show
1967	France launches nuclear submarine

EVENTS

1945	World War II ends with Hitler's suicide
1945	Atom bombs dropped on Hiroshima and Nagasaki
1947	US pilot Chuck Yeager breaks the sound barrier
1948	South Africa's Nationalist party comes to power and imposes apartheid
1949	NATO formed

1950	North Korea invades South Korea
1953	Francis Crick and James Watson discover the structure of DNA
1953	Edmund Hillary of New Zealand and Tenzing Norgay of Nepal climb Everest
1954	UK athlete Roger Bannister runs a mile in under four minutes
1955	Disneyland opens in California, US

1961	Cosmonaut Yuri Gagarin becomes the first man in space
1961	East German wall divides the city of Berlin
1963	US president John F. Kennedy assassinated
1967	Six-Day War in Israel
1967	Christiaan Barnard performs first heart transplant in South Africa
1969	First man lands on the Moon.

1970

We should all be concerned about the future because we will have to spend the rest of our lives there

C. F. KETTERING

FLOPPY DISC
Computer users in the 1970s were able to record data and install programmes using discs that were literally floppy. Information is now often stored on compact discs (CDs).

780863 185779

BAR CODE
Information can be quickly entered into a computer using a bar code. Bar codes have revolutionized supermarket checkouts where the scanner reads the product labels.

CONCORDE
Since 1976, Concorde – a joint project by British and French Airways – has flown at supersonic speeds across the Atlantic. It is criticized mainly for its noise pollution.

BRITISH AIRWAYS

Concorde taxiing

1980

Science fiction is a kind of archaeology of the future

CLIFTON FADIMAN

SPACE SHUTTLE
The space shuttle is the first reusable manned spacecraft. The first four space shuttles were named after famous ships, *Columbia*, *Challenger*, *Endeavour*, and *Atlantis*, reminding us how much humankind loves to explore.

Antenna

MOBILE PHONE
Our ability to make immediate contact with each other regardless of where we are is now taken for granted. Lightweight mobile telephones are becoming as familiar as wristwatches. Portable computers linked to telephones will allow access to the Internet in the future.

1990

Such abundance of fire and fiery missiles shall fall from the heavens that nothing shall escape the holocaust. And this will occur before the last conflagration – in 1999

NOSTRADAMUS

DESTINATION MARS
The *Pathfinder* probe landed on Mars on 4 July 1997. It released the *Sojourner*, a wheeled vehicle, which explored the Martian landscape. NASA is now making preparations to send the first astronauts to the red planet.

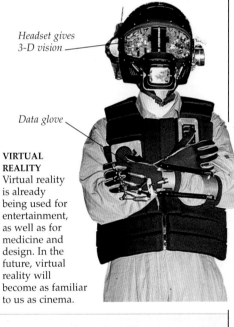

Headset gives 3-D vision

Data glove

VIRTUAL REALITY
Virtual reality is already being used for entertainment, as well as for medicine and design. In the future, virtual reality will become as familiar to us as cinema.

1970 IBM create the first floppy disc
1971 Food processor invented in France
1971 Soviet Union puts space station into orbit
1972 CT scanner introduced by UK researcher Godfrey Hounsfield
1976 Supersonic airliner Concorde makes first commercial flight
1979 Catalytic converter developed in UK

1981 World's first space shuttle US *Columbia* blasts off
1981 Stealth fighter plane has maiden flight in US
1982 First artificial heart implanted in US
1984 Genetic fingerprinting introduced
1985 Desktop (DTP) publishing created
1985 Mobile phones launched in Europe

1990 Sony produces Data Discman, an electronic book
1991 ERS-1, Europe's first environmental satellite, goes into orbit
1992 Virtual reality is developed as a 3-D video game in the US
1993 First voice-operated TV/radio remote control is launched

---

1973 Australia's Sydney Opera House completed amid controversy
1973 Last US troops leave Vietnam, but war does not end for two years
1974 Bar codes first introduced on products for sale in US
1979 Nuclear accident at Three Mile Island, Pennsylvania, US

1980 Mount St Helens erupts in the USA
1982 Argentine forces surrender Falkland Islands to UK
1985 Live Aid concert watched by 1.5 million people
1986 Space shuttle *Challenger* explodes
1986 Major nuclear accident at Chernobyl
1989 Berlin wall torn down

1990 BSE leads to beef ban on UK imports
1990 Saddam Hussein of Iraq invades Kuwait
1991 Civil war breaks out in Yugoslavia
1992 Hole in ozone layer stretches over the coast of South America for the first time
1994 ANC leader Nelson Mandela elected as first black president of South Africa
1997 *Pathfinder* probe lands on Mars

Our shrinking planet

THE WORLD IS GETTING SMALLER, or so it seems. Today, around 150 communication satellites in geostationary orbit the Earth, gathering information and enabling us to communicate with each other. Mobile phones, fax machines, and electronic mail keep us in touch wherever we are. Instant news reports, from cultural events to wars and famine, are routinely transmitted into our homes. The Internet, which began as a modest communications network between a number of universities, now has millions of users all over the world. Different strands of technology are starting to converge, and soon televisions, telephones, and computers will merge to become one technology. Access to doctors and other experts from all over the world will be available via video conferencing. However, this picture of worldwide communications can be misleading, as two-thirds of the world considers it a luxury to own a phone, let alone a personal computer. Information technology could benefit the entire world, but how long will it be before access to it becomes truly global?

GETTING WIRED
Technology has certainly come a long way since this group shared a moment listening to the latest sound recording! Via the Internet, it is now possible to connect to sites all over the world and share information – and music – with people from many different cultures.

Colours show traffic of information across the USA

DATA TRAFFIC
Today, users are connected by information superhighways. Networks like this one in the USA provide scientists at their own computers with access to much more powerful computers. This is a relatively small network, but the World Wide Web is global.

SENDING AND RECEIVING MESSAGES
The first satellite, *Sputnik 1*, was launched in 1957. Since then over two thousand more have been sent into space, although only a fraction of them are operating today. On the ground all around the world, satellite dishes (left) transmit and receive news and information. Around the Earth, many different countries have put into orbit geostationary communications satellites such as the *Intelsat K* (above right), and television satellites such as the *TDF-1* (right).

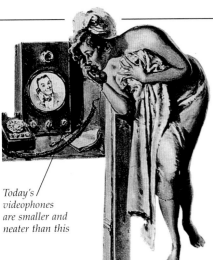

Today's videophones are smaller and neater than this

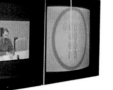

SEE MORE OF YOUR FRIENDS
This comical image from a 1956 magazine illustrates how people believe that having a videophone will invade privacy. It was not until the 1990s that technological advances made these machines a practical possibility.

FACE TO FACE
Video conferencing is already a popular form of communication among international businesses because it saves the time and expense of travel. Business people can hold meetings face-to-face, even though they may live and work at opposite ends of the globe. The system is already being used in schools. In the future, experts from all over the world will be invited "into the classroom" to lecture or give masterclasses, and answer the pupils' questions.

Equipment allows consultant to be "virtually present" at scene of accident

Headset is fitted with video camera, television screen, and voice microphone

Consultant views images sent from paramedic's camera and gives medical advice

A panel of solar cells collects and stores energy until someone wants to make a call

SAVING LIVES
It will not be long before a paramedic will be able to receive on-the-spot expert advice at the scene of an accident. The paramedic will be able to look at a diagram showing him or her exactly what to do. The life-saving equipment is a combination of video conferencing software and a satellite communications network.

SOLAR TELEPHONES
Many places around the world have no electricity. Solar power may provide the answer. This solar-powered telephone kiosk uses the sun to generate enough energy to transmit and receive calls.

FIBRE OPTICS
Flexible, thread-like strands of the purest glass have replaced copper wire in the cables used to transmit telephone and television signals. They can carry much more information and are specially treated so there is the minimum of distortion. This means high volumes of images or telephone conversations can be carried. There are now hundreds of thousands of kilometres of fibre optic cables around the globe.

A fibre the same thickness as a human hair can carry around one million conversations simultaneously

Watching the Earth

1 THE BLUE PLANET
In the 1960s, satellites and astronauts sent back the first pictures of our planet from space. From a long distance, our planet is predominately blue and, compared with the giant scale of the Universe, looks small and fragile.

HAVE YOU EVER WONDERED what your house looks like from space? Well, soon you will be able to find out. Satellite imaging is becoming so sophisticated that it is now possible to see every square metre of Earth from deep in space. One day in the future, not only will you be able to see your own house from space, you will even be able to see a newspaper left out on the lawn. The author George Orwell (1903-50) predicted a future in which our every move would be monitored by governments obsessed with control. In some ways he was right. Today, satellites watch us from space, and video cameras record our movements in shopping centres and other public places. But satellites have a variety of other useful purposes. Views of the Earth from the *Landsat* satellite provide us with vital ecological information. Satellites can also inform us of changes in urban and environmental conditions, and warn us in advance of any major ecological problem threatening the Earth.

BIG BROTHER IS WATCHING YOU
George Orwell's gloomy novel of the future, *Nineteen Eighty-Four*, predicted a society dominated by state control. Video screens not only provided constant propaganda, but were also linked to surveillance cameras. Terrified citizens were rarely out of the sight of "Big Brother".

3 MOVING CLOSER
Zooming in even closer, it is possible to see further detail. In the north of Italy, the southern Alps mountain range comes into focus. The pictures have been produced by taking thousands of satellite images and piecing them together with a computer. Using cameras that are able to home in to provide close detail, it is possible to see a small area of a continent.

2 CLOUDLESS SKIES OVER EUROPE
With today's technology, satellites out in space can pinpoint particular details on Earth such as expanses of vegetation, large rivers, deserts, and huge mountain ranges. But in order to do this, it is essential that the satellite's view is not obscured by thick layers of clouds. This sequence has been put together with cloudless images taken by satellite.

Cloudless image of Italy

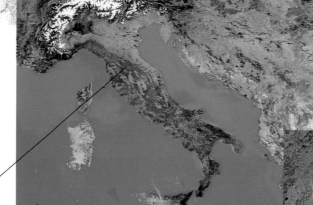

Eye of the storm at the heart of the hurricane

Southern Alps mountain range

4 MOUNTAIN SCENERY
The snowcapped ridges of the mountain range come into view. So far, this photographic technique has been used only by the military of various countries, but will soon be available for commercial purposes. It will be possible to own pictures of your house taken from space.

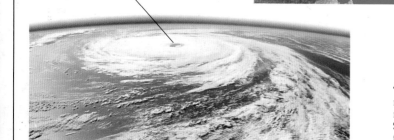

WATCHING THE WEATHER
Satellites and spacecraft allow meteorologists to monitor weather conditions on Earth. This view from the *Atlantis* space shuttle shows Hurricane Florence in 1988 as it swept dangerously across the Atlantic Ocean. Weather satellites in orbit can see how clouds are moving, and weather forecasters use this information to predict the weather.

View of the city centre of Washington DC, in the USA

EYE IN THE SKY
The first *Landsat* satellite was launched in 1974 to monitor changes on Earth. Since then, four successors have been launched, each providing increasingly detailed data about urban areas, deforestation, pollution, and natural disasters.

Highest ozone concentration

TEMPERATURE TRENDS
These computer-generated maps show world temperature trends. The evidence suggests that temperatures will increase considerably in the 21st century, which many believe to be an indication of global warming. If this is the case, the consequences will be devastating for many parts of the world.

OZONE DEPLETION
The ozone layer shields Earth from the Sun's harmful ultraviolet rays, but certain gases are depleting the protective layer. This picture (left) shows the ozone hole over Antarctica. The colours show ozone concentration from dark red for the lowest to green for the highest.

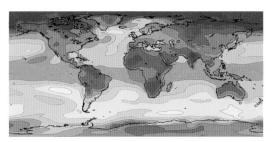

Predicted temperatures for 2050

-1   0   1   2   3   4   5

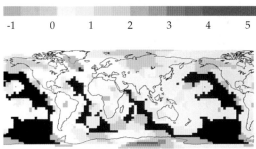

Temperature trends 1965-1985

-3 -2 -1 0 1 2 3 4 5

5 IN DETAIL
It is now possible to see clearly the details of the thick vegetation in the valleys between the high mountains in the range. At this distance, we can make out the courses the rivers follow and how much snow covers the giant mountain-tops.

Contours of the rivers

6 HOMING IN
Satellite imaging is able to focus on a 1-m (3-ft) area. So, from space it is possible to take pictures of a rock on the face of the Matterhorn. In the future, image systems may even take us underground or allow us to explore the deepest depths of the oceans.

3-D image of Matterhorn

A growing world

THE WORLD'S POPULATION IS GROWING at an incredible rate. In the last 200 years it has accelerated from about one billion to over six billion, and is only now beginning to show signs of slowing down. The birth rate is higher than the death rate and, according to the social scientists who study population trends, these rates are unlikely to balance out until the world population reaches 10 or 11 billion. With advanced medical care, improved living conditions, and a healthier diet in the future, we will live longer, be more active, and have a better quality of life. But if the planet is to sustain such a high population, it will be necessary to preserve and protect its natural resources. Nations will have to work together to reduce pollution, protect the forests, control pesticides, and find alternative sources of energy to fossil fuels.

TOO MANY MOUTHS TO FEED
Overpopulation puts a strain on resources. In many countries, a natural disaster, such as flooding or crop failure, already causes famine. The lack of clean drinking water or an inadequate supply of food will devastate entire communities.

GETTING OLDER
Improved medical care, a better diet, and a healthier lifestyle lead not only to a longer life, but also to a fitter one. Because of this, it is likely that many people will live to the age of 100 or more from the beginning of the 21st century.

GROWING POPULATION
In just over a century, the world's population has tripled in size. Up until the early 1800s, the population remained under one billion. However, better health and living conditions resulted in the birth rate exceeding the death rate, and by 1900, there were two billion people in the world. Less than 50 years later, the population reached three billion. Today, it has reached more than six billion, and is expected to continue to rise at a rate of about one billion every 12 years. This chart shows the dramatic rise in billions from 1800, showing how the numbers are likely to become stable from 2100 onwards.

Population in billions

1800	1850	1900	1950	2000	2050	2100	2150

Year

12
11
10
9
8
7
6
5
4
3
2
1

CITY SPRAWL
More and more of the world's population is now concentrated in urban areas. Cities with a million inhabitants are commonplace, and some exceed this – the metropolitan area of Tokyo, Japan, already has a population of over 29 million. Today, 37 per cent of the population of developing countries lives in cities, and this figure is expected to rise, increasing the pressure to provide jobs, housing, and public services.

POLLUTED ATMOSPHERE

We consume billions of tonnes of fossil fuels every year, using up natural resources and polluting the atmosphere. The exhaust fumes from motor vehicles, together with emissions from factories, produce noxious smogs that have catastrophic consequences both for people's health and for the environment.

Power station in Moscow

THIRST FOR FOREIGN CULTURE

Certain cultures have become more attractive and desirable than others. The American way of life has a huge impact on the desire for consumer goods throughout the world. In the future, such a demand for consumer goods may deplete our natural resources.

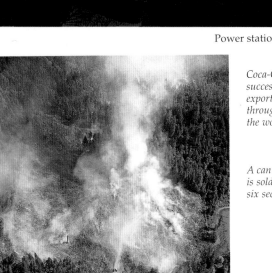

Coca-Cola is successfully exported throughout the world

A can of coke is sold every six seconds

Slum dwellings lie not far from modern buildings in Sao Paulo, Brazil

CONSERVING OUR FUTURE

The high demand for timber and agricultural land has meant that vast tracts of South American jungle are being lost forever. This has a devastating effect on plants and animals, and causes enormous damage to the Earth's atmosphere. Governments must promote better agricultural practices before it is too late.

GROWTH OF DEVELOPING COUNTRIES

When poor agricultural workers migrate from the countryside to urban areas they put a great strain on the work market, housing, and public services – the city's infrastructure. Around 37 per cent of the population of developing countries live in cities, and this figure is expected to rise to 50 per cent in the next few years.

Environment friendly

Technological progress has provided us with many advantages, and will continue to do so in the future. But there is a price to pay – the damaged ozone layer and the effects of greenhouse gases may have terrible consequences for the future of our planet. Air pollution is causing acid rain, and water contamination is killing wildlife. Some natural resources are rapidly being used up, and many large tracts of rainforest have been destroyed. Because of our actions, some of the animals we shared the planet with are extinct, while others are endangered. If we do not take a more responsible attitude towards our finite resources, the results will be catastrophic.

VISIONS OF THE FUTURE
Creating your own artificially controlled environment once seemed an exciting prospect. Some architects have taken great pleasure in designing future homes, such as this one from the 1950s, which rotates to face any direction. Protected by a climate-conditioned dome, it would be possible to enjoy summer activities in the middle of winter. Such schemes can be seen today in holiday parks and leisure centres.

IDEAL FOR THE CITY OF THE FUTURE
The motor car is a very popular form of transportation. But people are concerned at the levels of pollution and the future scarcity of petrol. Manufacturers are therefore designing cars for city use with clean, fuel-efficient engines.

ALTERNATIVE TO FUEL
Scientists around the world are searching for alternatives to non-renewable and expensive fossil fuels. Alcohol, which is made from distilled grain, is one alternative to petrol. It has been a success in countries without natural oil reserves.

Lightweight body means engine has to do less work and so requires less fuel

Honda's solar car in the World Solar Challenge Race

POWERED BY THE SUN
A solar-powered vehicle uses solar cells to convert energy from the sun into electricity, which drives its electric motors. Yet solar cars are still little more than expensive novelties. However, solar cells are likely to play a major role in the future generation of electricity.

SOLAR POWER STATION
Solar energy has enormous potential, but it is costly to collect and difficult to convert and store. Flat-plate collectors are used in some homes for heating water, but because of the relatively low temperatures produced, it is not practical to convert the heat energy into electricity. Concentrating collectors (left) can focus sunlight onto a single target and generate high temperatures to power steam turbine electric generators. A computer turns the dish to make sure it faces the sun throughout the day.

Streamlined shape prevents wind traps

Building supported by giant tripod megastructure

RECYCLING

Increasingly, people are becoming aware of the value of recycling. Today, we generate an enormous amount of waste, and there are increasing problems with its disposal. In the future, we will manufacture products that are built to last, and can be repaired. They will be easily dismantled for sometimes surprising reuse (right), or at least disposed of safely and efficiently.

Worn rubber tyres are not safe to use

Tyre ready to be re-formed after shredding

Handbag made from shredded car tyre

OFFICES IN THE 21ST CENTURY

Most traditional offices are not environmentally friendly. They consume high levels of energy in winter, and require even more to keep them cool in summer. They often lack a natural source of air and light, and so need electric lighting switched on all day. This not only results in high fuel costs, but is also unpleasant for the occupants. As the cost of fuels rises, energy-inefficient office buildings will need to be redesigned. This remarkable-looking office building has been designed to address exactly these problems – maximizing the use of both natural ventilation and light.

Hot, stale air ventilates through louvre at the top of the building

In winter, warm air at the top is used to heat cold air coming in at the bottom

Air between glass skins is heated by solar radiation

Mirrors reflect natural light deep into offices

Air-conditioning is replaced by a natural ventilation system

Building stands high above ground, away from pollution

Continued from previous page

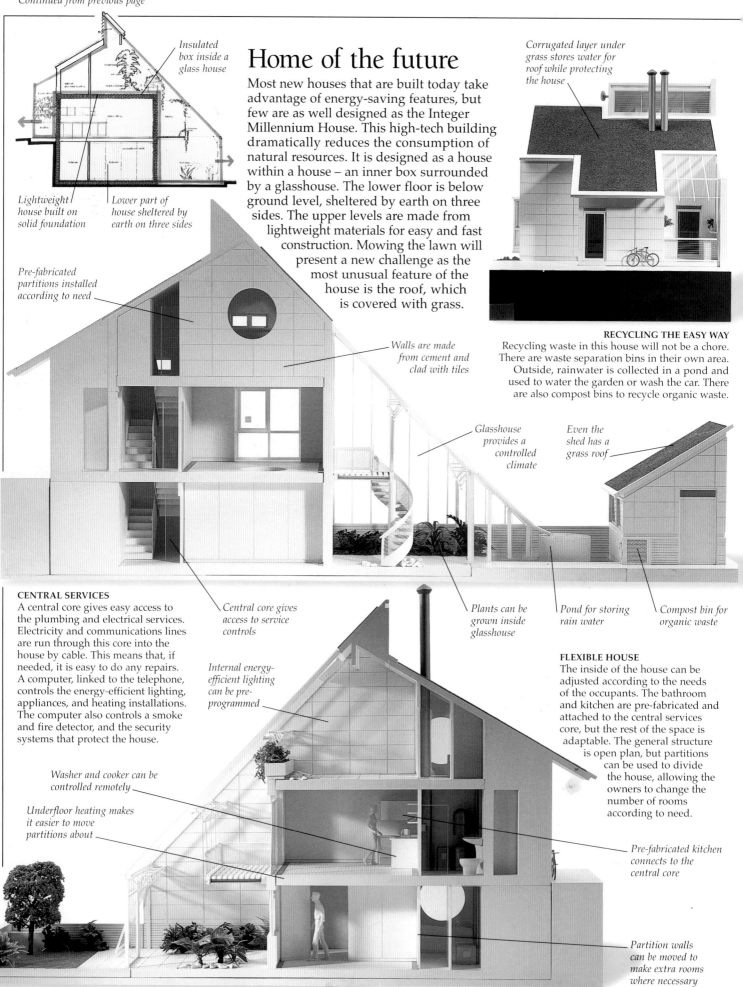

Insulated box inside a glass house

Lightweight house built on solid foundation

Lower part of house sheltered by earth on three sides

Home of the future

Most new houses that are built today take advantage of energy-saving features, but few are as well designed as the Integer Millennium House. This high-tech building dramatically reduces the consumption of natural resources. It is designed as a house within a house – an inner box surrounded by a glasshouse. The lower floor is below ground level, sheltered by earth on three sides. The upper levels are made from lightweight materials for easy and fast construction. Mowing the lawn will present a new challenge as the most unusual feature of the house is the roof, which is covered with grass.

Corrugated layer under grass stores water for roof while protecting the house

RECYCLING THE EASY WAY
Recycling waste in this house will not be a chore. There are waste separation bins in their own area. Outside, rainwater is collected in a pond and used to water the garden or wash the car. There are also compost bins to recycle organic waste.

Pre-fabricated partitions installed according to need

Walls are made from cement and clad with tiles

Glasshouse provides a controlled climate

Even the shed has a grass roof

CENTRAL SERVICES
A central core gives easy access to the plumbing and electrical services. Electricity and communications lines are run through this core into the house by cable. This means that, if needed, it is easy to do any repairs. A computer, linked to the telephone, controls the energy-efficient lighting, appliances, and heating installations. The computer also controls a smoke and fire detector, and the security systems that protect the house.

Central core gives access to service controls

Plants can be grown inside glasshouse

Pond for storing rain water

Compost bin for organic waste

FLEXIBLE HOUSE
The inside of the house can be adjusted according to the needs of the occupants. The bathroom and kitchen are pre-fabricated and attached to the central services core, but the rest of the space is adaptable. The general structure is open plan, but partitions can be used to divide the house, allowing the owners to change the number of rooms according to need.

Internal energy-efficient lighting can be pre-programmed

Washer and cooker can be controlled remotely

Underfloor heating makes it easier to move partitions about

Pre-fabricated kitchen connects to the central core

Partition walls can be moved to make extra rooms where necessary

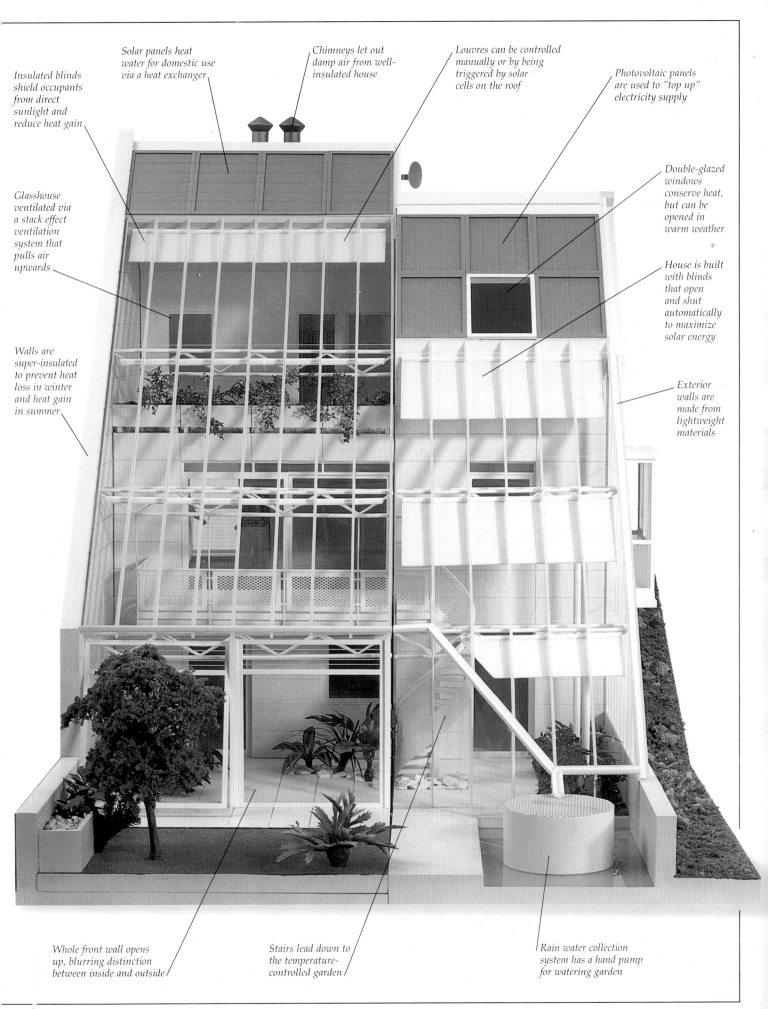

Insulated blinds shield occupants from direct sunlight and reduce heat gain

Solar panels heat water for domestic use via a heat exchanger

Chimneys let out damp air from well-insulated house

Louvres can be controlled manually or by being triggered by solar cells on the roof

Photovoltaic panels are used to "top up" electricity supply

Glasshouse ventilated via a stack effect ventilation system that pulls air upwards

Double-glazed windows conserve heat, but can be opened in warm weather

House is built with blinds that open and shut automatically to maximize solar energy

Walls are super-insulated to prevent heat loss in winter and heat gain in summer

Exterior walls are made from lightweight materials

Whole front wall opens up, blurring distinction between inside and outside

Stairs lead down to the temperature-controlled garden

Rain water collection system has a hand pump for watering garden

Futuropolis

PEOPLE ARE ATTRACTED to living in cities because of the cultural and economic opportunities they offer. It will not be long before most people become urban dwellers. It will be necessary to build new cities and rebuild existing cities to accommodate the huge increase in the world's population. These cities will need to be very carefully planned, and existing transport systems will have to be redesigned. High-rise offices and apartment towers, taller than ever before, will become self-contained, with their own shops, restaurants, and leisure facilities. They will operate in a similar way to small towns, and the occupants will rarely need to leave them. The pollution caused by increased numbers of people will need to be managed, so the combustion engine will be banned, and buildings will be energy-efficient, making use of renewable energy.

CITY-BUILDING FOR THE NEW MILLENNIUM

One answer to potential overcrowding is to build upwards, constructing huge structures like the proposed Millennium Tower, to be built in Daiba Bay, Tokyo, Japan, in the early 21st century. The tower will be a self-contained township 150 stories high, with a population of 50,000. High-speed double-decker lifts will carry 80 people at a time to "sky centres", where they can visit restaurants and shops, or enjoy all forms of entertainment, including the cinema or discos. From the sky centres, residents will travel by conventional high-speed lifts to their flats or places of work on the other floors.

840 m
(2,755 ft)

451.9 m
(1,483 ft)

381 m
(1,250 ft)

Millennium Tower

Petronas Towers

Empire State Building

Towers can withstand high winds and earthquakes

FLYING CITIES

This is how one visionary of 1929 saw New York in the future – as a travelling city suspended high above the ground. The nearest we are likely to come to cities in the sky are spaceships that will orbit the Earth.

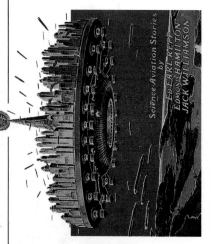

Science and Aviation Stories
by
ED EARL REPP
EDMOND HAMILTON
JACK WILLIAMSON

BUILDING HIGH

Today's Manhattan skyline demonstrates one architectural solution to the lack of space. Some of the world's tallest buildings are among those that crowd the island city of New York. The high price of land in the city encouraged architects to construct tall steel-framed skyscrapers on small lots.

Empire State Building

Honeycomb hotel rooms in Tokyo, Japan

HOTELS OF THE FUTURE

Huge numbers of Japanese commuters often need to stay in Tokyo's extraordinary space-saving hotels overnight. Each individual sleeps in a capsule that is air-conditioned and equipped with a television and washing facilities.

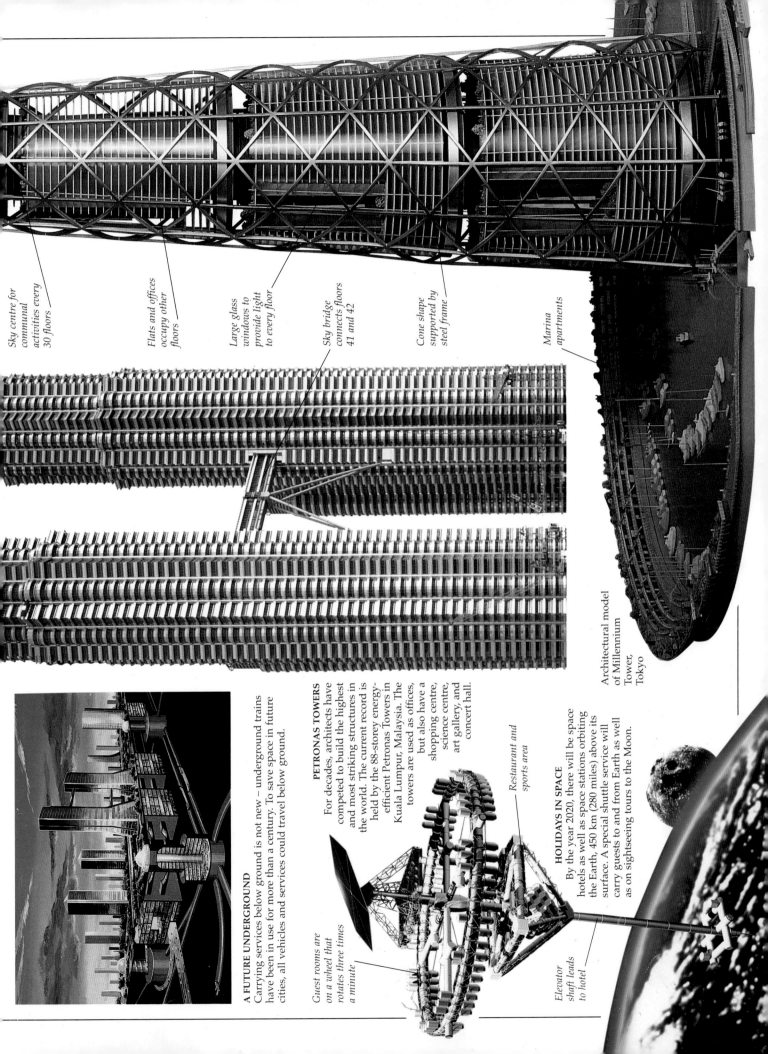

Sky centre for communal activities every 30 floors

Flats and offices occupy other floors

Large glass windows to provide light to every floor

Sky bridge connects floors 41 and 42

Cone shape supported by steel frame

Marina apartments

Architectural model of Millennium Tower, Tokyo

A FUTURE UNDERGROUND

Carrying services below ground is not new – underground trains have been in use for more than a century. To save space in future cities, all vehicles and services could travel below ground.

PETRONAS TOWERS

For decades, architects have competed to build the highest and most striking structures in the world. The current record is held by the 88-storey energy-efficient Petronas Towers in Kuala Lumpur, Malaysia. The towers are used as offices, but also have a shopping centre, science centre, art gallery, and concert hall.

Guest rooms are on a wheel that rotates three times a minute

Restaurant and sports area

HOLIDAYS IN SPACE

By the year 2020, there will be space hotels as well as space stations orbiting the Earth, 450 km (280 miles) above its surface. A special shuttle service will carry guests to and from Earth as well as on sightseeing tours to the Moon.

Elevator shaft leads to hotel

Getting control

THE FREEDOM TO TRAVEL IS VALUED highly, yet it is essential that we reduce fuel consumption, control pollution, and manage our busy roads. In the future, all journeys will be planned in advance for optimum efficiency. By displaying the position of the car on a digital map, a satellite-linked navigation system will make sure that drivers know their exact location. They will simply indicate their desired destination, and the car will provide detailed instructions on the best way to get there. A powerful onboard computer will monitor the car's movements, and will take action, such as turning off the engine if erratic driving indicates that the driver is about to fall asleep. On long-distance journeys, it will be possible to drive on an automated highway where the car will travel in a convoy, its speed and steering controlled by the computer. In the air, improved tracking systems will mean that more aircraft can travel safely at closer distances. The Future Air Navigational System (FANS) will allow pilots to switch routes to take advantage of jet streams, which will speed up travel across the world, as well as saving on fuel.

ACCURATE PREDICTION
As early as 1919, it was already obvious that the number of cars in densely populated cities was going to cause parking problems. The suggested solution, a multi-storey car park, is now a familiar sight. Unfortunately, building more car parks may only encourage more cars on the road.

Car is powered by electricity controlled by electronics

ELECTRICAL HIGHWAY
This advertisement from the 1950s suggests a future free of accidents and traffic jams. A car would be propelled along an electrical superhighway, its speed and steering controlled by electronic devices embedded in the road. The family would just sit back, playing board games and enjoying the journey.

AUTOMATED HIGHWAY
Today the automated highway is becoming a reality. Experiments are taking place with cars that can steer, accelerate, and brake by themselves. They are fitted with computers that pick up signals from magnets set in the road. They will travel in convoy along designated stretches of motorways.

Using this computer simulation, researchers can predict the behaviour of drivers under different conditions

THE FUTREX MONORAIL
A US company has developed a revolutionary new monorail transport system nicknamed "The Beam". The carriages are hung on the side of the rail, rather than on top, so the monorail can travel both ways on either side of the beam.

The system is capable of carrying around 12,000 passengers per hour

Radar screen identifies each aircraft

Arrow on screen indicates the direction in which to drive

BEING GIVEN THE ALL CLEAR
Like the roads, the skies are becoming overcrowded, and serious accidents can happen while planes taxi to and from the runway. A new generation of radar systems, combined with powerful computers, track and predict aircraft movements in advance, making it easier for traffic controllers to select flight paths. The new safety systems will control the location of all aircraft, whether they are on the ground or in the air.

IN-CAR NAVIGATION SYSTEM
Imagine driving a car that never lets you get lost. There will soon be onboard mapping facilities in all new cars. This system (right) uses a CD-ROM to store maps, and its aerial receives location signals via global positioning satellites. The driver types in the destination, the computer works out the best route, and a digitized voice provides instructions on how to get there.

UNJAMMING THE TRAFFIC
The reasons for traffic jams are complex. There are too many cars on the roads, but simply building more roads is not the answer. Instead, planners are using the latest computer technology to predict with greater accuracy the reasons for traffic jams. The simulation of traffic patterns (left) takes into account a variety of factors affecting the actual traffic (right). These factors include changing weather conditions, different types of vehicles and driving styles, breakdowns, and accidents. This information is studied to increase the road network, control traffic speeds, and provide alternative routes.

This analysis shows the flow of traffic on a busy highway intersection in the USA

Getting around

OUR DESIRE TO TRAVEL will not diminish in the 21st century, indeed it is likely to increase. More people will own cars so roads will become more congested. We will want to move around the world more quickly, but the skies are already in danger of becoming crowded with aircraft. Attention is now focussing on how to ease these potential problems (pp. 24-25). Train travel will be faster and much more economical to operate, providing passengers and freight with an alternative to jammed motorways. And giant aeroplanes that travel at hypersonic speeds – five times faster than Concorde – may one day take passengers around the world in a fraction of the time it takes today.

BEAT THE TRAFFIC
This 1923 illustration solves future problems of urban congestion by using "torpedo" cars to carry passengers above the busy streets.

Computers calculate the optimum tilt angle in relation to speed

Front wheels and body tilt during cornering

Sensor-controlled headlamp switches on automatically

SAILING ON A WING
Ships will probably continue to be the most reliable means of transporting any commercial goods from continent to continent. But shippers are still looking for ways of cutting back on fuel consumption. Some tankers and yachts have already been equipped with computer-controlled wingsails. These unusual-looking sails can save on fuel costs. They are able to survive hurricanes at sea with wind speeds of 100 knots.

Electricity provided by solar panels

CAR OF THE FUTURE
This lightweight three-wheeler is designed for a driver and one passenger, making it an ideal car for the city. It has an onboard computer that calculates the highest cornering speeds, and the front wheels and body lean when the car is cornering. This provides the maximum speed in the greatest safety and comfort. To add to the fun, the roof can be removed and stored away.

Roof is stored in a compartment above rear wheel

Jet-style steering wheel

Lightweight aluminium bodywork

Special tread tyres designed for low friction

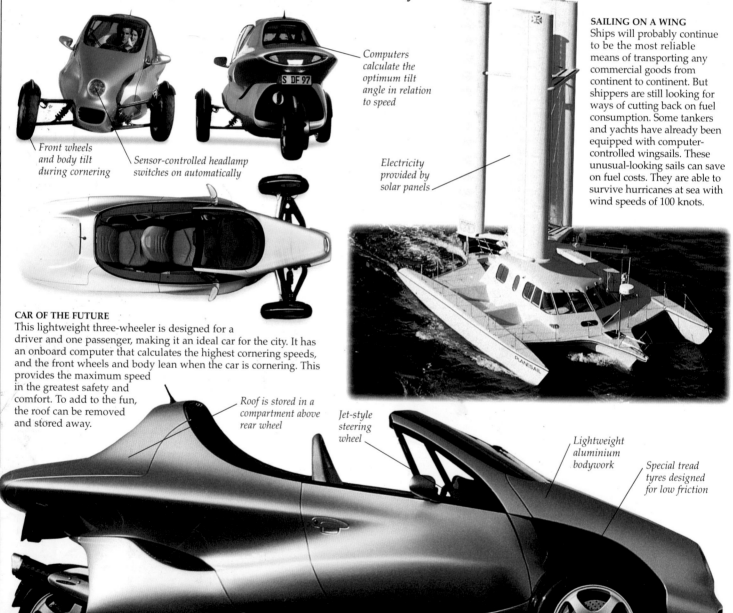

Turbofan
engines

Folding
fore-wings

FLYING HYPERSONICALLY
Supersonic travel has been possible for transatlantic passengers since the mid-1970s when the British and French built Concorde. NASA are now developing the Hyper-X to fly at hypersonic speeds – five times faster than the speed of sound. It will be unpiloted, and launched from a B52 aircraft. Other countries are developing larger and faster versions for the 21st century.

Helicopter-style
rotors

Turboprop
engine

FLYING HIGH
The tiltrotor takes off like a helicopter but flies like a plane. Its wings have helicopter-style rotors, which can be raised into a vertical or forward position for take-off. The tiltrotor would be particularly useful in urban environments, and a passenger version for commercial, short-haul flights will become a popular form of transport in the early 21st century.

LEVITATED TRAVEL
High-Speed Surface Transport (HSST) may be the most practical means of moving large numbers of people to their destinations quickly and economically. This Maglev train is being developed in Japan. It is magnetically levitated, which means it does not travel on wheels. Instead, a high-strength magnetic field enables it to glide over the surface of the monorail track at speeds of over 200 km/h (125 mph).

Monorail
guideway

Cars travel on
"airways" at
different levels

TAKING TO THE SKIES
The mass use of private aircraft has never been a very practical proposition. As roads become more congested, we may be forced to take to the skies. But it is unlikely that cities of the future will be filled with flying cars as imagined for the science fiction film *The Fifth Element* (1997).

Passenger
entrance

WHEN IS A CAR NOT A CAR?
Concept 2096 is truly a vehicle of the future. This "idea" does not have wheels. Instead, it has a revolutionary "slug drive" motion (yet to be invented) that propels the vehicle at speeds of 480 km/h (300 mph), dramatically cutting down travelling time. It is driven by a navigational computer, so there is no need for a driver, brakes, or steering wheel. With a vehicle like this, pollution will be a thing of the past. It uses re-chargeable fuel cells, a clean substitute for petrol and diesel.

Concept 2096 can
change shape
and colour

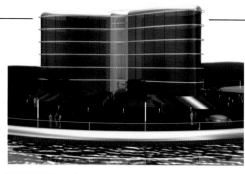

IDEAL HOME
By the year 2020, some of us might be lucky enough to live in homes with all the latest technology. These will be built from hard-wearing materials that require little maintenance. Fully automated, homes will react to changes in the weather, the heating controls adjusting to outside temperatures.

Virtually home in 2020

HOMES OF THE FUTURE will be very different places from those of the 20th century. They will be energy efficient and simple to clean and maintain. They will have access to the outside world via a global communications network, making it easy to run a business, do the shopping, and plan a winter holiday, all from the comfort of a living room. There will be an integrated management system, with heating, lighting, and security controls that react to the needs of the occupants. The walls will be constructed from new interactive materials that are able to change appearance at the touch of a button to suit a particular mood, while high-resolution wrap-around video screens and holographic projectors will provide fun and entertainment for the whole family.

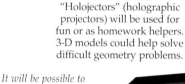

HOMEWORK HELPER
"Holojectors" (holographic projectors) will be used for fun or as homework helpers. 3-D models could help solve difficult geometry problems.

Scanner in walls of shower connects to health centre

POWER SHOWER
A health and hygiene station will scan and monitor your well-being while you shower. It will be linked directly to a health centre that has a complete record of your family's medical history.

It will be possible to have holographic master classes

SOMETHING FOR EVERYONE
The dining table will have a multitude of uses. Linked to a communications system, its screens will display personalized electronic newspapers, and allow you to make contact with distant friends and family while you eat.

Interactive screen

Interactive on-line book with flexible screen

"IT'S GOOD TO TALK"
Portable telephones will still be used for business and pleasure, but by the year 2020 they will all be videophones. Increased bandwidth will allow more and more digital information to be sent over the airwaves.

High-resolution video image

Nanorobots the size of spiders will roam the carpets, keeping them clean and free of dust

Furniture will be made of special self-cleaning materials

RELAXATION SERVICE
The future family will be able to relax using a therapy couch. Sensitive arms and rollers will gently massage tired body parts, easing away aches and pains. The couch will be linked to a special physiotherapy service, which will give expert advice on health, diet, and exercise.

Screen displays advice

Massage rollers move the length of the couch

Virtual station combines thought control technology with artificial sensory feedback

WRIST SET
Unlike conventional watches, which only tell the time and date, or do simple computing tasks, this wrist set will access information to suit a particular interest, for example, the sports results or traffic news. Such functional electronic gadgets may even replace traditional decorative jewellery.

Clip-on wrist band

VIRTUAL REALITY TRAINER
The 2020 home will have its own virtual reality machine. With this, the family will be able to practice dangerous sports such as mountain climbing or bungee jumping, or visit exotic locations on a virtual holiday at the touch of a button.

Walls of house change image to suit mood

VR HEADSETS
In the future, headsets linked to camcorder technology will be able to record your experiences with stereo sound. Using virtual reality headsets, it will be possible to experience 3-D images for pleasure, learning, or business.

Thought recognition sensors

WORK STATION
Working from home is already a popular alternative for many people. In the future, small work stations will provide full access to everything needed to conduct daily business affairs, from e-mail to video conferencing.

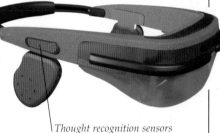

Single function robots have already been prototyped

ROBOT SERVANTS
Imagine having an addition to the household that always does what it is told. Single function robots such as vacuum cleaners or lawn trimmers will perform simple tasks around the home. A drinks table that comes to you when it is called will certainly be useful, but it will be better still if it takes away dirty glasses and loads them in the dishwasher.

Chair-based work stations will replace the traditional office

SHOP FROM HOME
Shopping from home has been possible for some time, first through mail-order and then through television. It is only recently that Internet shopping has become popular, although it is not quite like the 1950s image of the future pictured here.

Easy living

IMAGINE STANDING AT a bus stop when suddenly your "hot badge" signals that the person behind you likes the same music. This might be all you need to know to start a conversation and become friends. Our everyday lives may soon be changed forever because of clever inventions like this one. Emotion containers will be filled with precious gifts, while an intelligent garbage can sorts out domestic rubbish. Friendly robots will learn how to perform simple tasks and will develop unique personalities. Some jobs, such as shopping or going to the bank, can already be done from home on the Internet, and soon we will be able to consult a doctor in the same way. Travel will be made more fun with electronic travel guides and "ear-ins" that translate foreign languages.

PULL-OUT TRAVEL GUIDE
In the future, finding your way around will be easier with this travel guide. It has a built-in destination planner and provides information about the country you are visiting. The information will be shown on a flexible pull-out screen.

Emotion containers can be any shape or size

Containers are decorative objects

EMOTION CONTAINERS
Emotion containers are precious gifts. They are pleasing to look at and are made from valuable materials. But they are much more than that. Each has a small screen, a loudspeaker, and a scent compartment. The giver of the gift captures a special moment – a clip from a home video or special film, or a baby's first words. They add a favourite scent and the moment is captured for the recipient to enjoy.

All you have to do is drop the rubbish in here

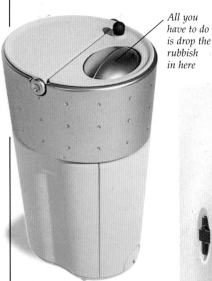

Videophone link with local doctor or hospital

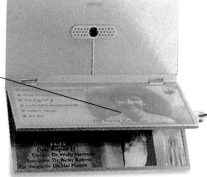

INTELLIGENT GARBAGE CAN
Recycling can be a problem, but in the future dealing with rubbish will be less messy. The intelligent garbage can is designed to sort rubbish, keep it from smelling, and make it into compact parcels ready for collection and recycling.

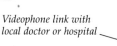

THE HOME MEDICAL BOX
The home medical box will check any symptoms of illness at home, while a hand-held computer helps to make a full medical diagnosis. The box has an electronic encyclopedia as well as instruments for measuring temperature, blood pressure, and heart rate. Information can be sent via video link to a local doctor or hospital so that expert medical advice can be given. The box also allows doctors to remotely monitor patients.

Hot badges glow when they "see" a friend

SMART CARDS

Cash will become a thing of the past; carrying smart cards in small wallets will be safer. Fingerprint or voice recognition technology will ensure the card can only be used by its owner. Small credit card sized screens will display personal photographs.

Video screen for photographs

MAKING FRIENDS

Hot badges will brighten up your social life. These short-range communication devices are loaded with all your personal information. They broadcast your personal profile and receive other badges' broadcast. If profiles match, the badges will signal their wearers.

EAR-INS

What if hot badges signal that you like the same music, but it turns out that you speak different languages? This will not matter with "ear-ins." These small devices fit snugly in the human ear and can translate simultaneously from one language to another.

Card carries all personal details

Flippin da traxx -
<<turn it up or turn it off>>

Touchpad

YOUR PERSONAL INTERNET

This gadget is designed for teenagers. It is a communications device that also gives access to entertainment, like music and videos, and information services, such as libraries. It will help with homework projects, but can also be used to communicate with friends.

This electronic pet will be able to respond to its owner with sound

Electronic pets can be any shape

ELECTRONIC PETS

When we think of robots, we tend to think of the functions they can perform. Robots that can do the washing and ironing or teach you how to play tennis have obvious advantages. But we rarely think of robots as cuddly friends. This is where these robots are different. They are designed to be companions rather than servants. They are capable of responding to emotional needs, and react to voice commands as well as touches or gestures. They have sensors, so they can become familiar with their homes. Like animal pets, they like to be loved.

All in the mind

BRAIN POWER
For centuries, scientists and philosophers believed that different mental activities could be attributed to specific regions of the brain, as in this 17th-century illustration. However, it is now clear that the regions often depend on each other. While one area of the brain may be crucial for vision, another may be needed to interpret visual information.

THE BRAIN IS THE MOST COMPLEX organ in the human body – and the least understood. Even with today's sophisticated medical technology, our knowledge of how it works remains basic. Physically, electrical brain waves can be measured using an electroencephalograph (EEG). Through a technique known as biofeedback, it is even possible to control and alter regular brain patterns. Changes in signal can then be used by a computer to operate electronic devices such as a television screen. The brain also stores our memories and governs our emotions. Understanding people's thoughts and feelings is still the subject of psychological theories such as psychoanalysis.

However, scientists are also exploring methods for recording life as we experience it through millions of tiny probes implanted in the brain and connected by radio to a computer. The possibility is that, one day, we will record all our thoughts and emotions. The data would then be downloaded, so that a person's experiences are stored for anybody to watch.

Sigmund Freud aged 65

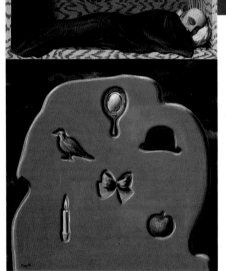

INTERPRETING DREAMS
Sigmund Freud (1856-1939) founded the science of psychoanalysis, a method of analysing and treating mental illness. He stated that our lives are influenced by both conscious and unconscious thoughts. He believed that through the interpretation of dreams we can have an insight into the unconscious mind.

DREAMS IN ART
Artists have often tried to express the mysteries of the mind through art. Surrealist artist René Magritte (1898-1967) used Freud's theories to explore the unconscious mind through painting.

Magritte's *The Reckless Sleeper* (1927)

SLEEP PATTERNS
There are two distinct types of sleep: rapid eye movement (REM) sleep and non-rapid eye movement (NREM) sleep. During REM, there is a great deal of eye, body, and brain activity associated with dreaming. During NREM sleep, eye, body, and brain activity varies. In deep sleep, breathing and heart rate slow down and the blood pressure drops. In the night, sleep patterns alternate between periods of REM and NREM.

Electrodes connected to monitoring machines measure brain activity

Brain activity in left hemisphere

Brain activity in right hemisphere

REM of left eye

REM of right eye

Heart activity

STEERING POWER

This woman is steering a flight simulator by the power of thought alone. Researchers have discovered that patterns of brain activity can be activated by pulsating lights. By using skilled biofeedback techniques, this particular scientist can control her brain's response to the lights. Increased brain activity turns the simulator plane right, reduced brain activity turns it left.

Green line indicates movement of plane against horizon

Scientist controls dial in simulator

Brain activity of scientist tunes into the rhythm of pulsating lights

PERSONALITY TRANSPLANT

This scene from the film *Batman Forever*, in which Jim Carrey receives a thought-wave transplant, may not be entirely imaginary. Scientists are developing a means of connecting nerve endings to microchips. One day, it may be possible to implant memory probes to record and store experiences.

Wearer lights up icon using his concentration

MIND OVER MATTER

Japanese scientists have produced a device that can detect changes in the beta waves produced by the mind when it is alert. These changes are picked-up, amplified, and sent to a computer, which is linked to a control panel. By learning to control the brain waves, it is possible to operate switches on anything from a television to a central heating system.

Electrode in goggles picks up changes in the beta waves

Different parts of the brain control different functions

INSIDE THE BRAIN

Today's advanced technology allows us to see right inside our own heads, and understand more about what is going on there. This computer generated view of a head with the "lid" taken off shows the parts of the brain that control most complex functions.

Understanding our bodies

THE HUMAN BODY HAS ALWAYS held mysteries, because for so long it was impossible to see exactly how it worked. Anatomists drew the first accurate diagrams from dissected corpses. Then, with the invention of X-rays, it became possible to see through living skin and muscle to the skeleton. Today, doctors use imaging technology to help them monitor patients and diagnose illnesses. Ultrasound is used to observe the progress of a growing foetus inside the womb. Magnetic Resonance Imaging (MRI) can build three-dimensional images of the interior of the body, allowing doctors to detect diseases. Today, advances in technology even show us the invisible! Electron microscopes allow us to look into a cell and see the structure of DNA. In the future we will have a complete record of our genetic make-up.

SUBJECT FOR STUDY
The skeleton is the only part of the human body that does not decay quickly after we die. It defines our shape, allows us to walk upright, and is the frame that supports our body. To understand how it worked, our ancestors had to cut up dead bodies to examine the bones.

Artwork of major organs within the muscular system

THE INNER PERSON
In 1895, German physicist Wilhelm Roentgen took an X-ray of his wife's hand. For the first time it was possible to look inside the body without cutting the skin. Today, X-rays allow doctors to see the condition of bones and ligaments.

A computer version of the traditional view of the venous system – the veins of the body – as one continuous vessel

Computer enhanced view of the skeletal muscular system

Computer generated image of the central nervous system

MAPPING THE BODY
New scanning techniques such as Magnetic Resonance Imaging (MRI) have made it possible to map the human body very accurately, unlike many of these representations. MRI allows doctors and surgeons to see soft tissue inside the body, such as the brain and spinal cord. By using a powerful magnetic force and radio waves, it is possible to produce a detailed three-dimensional image of the body to aid diagnosis.

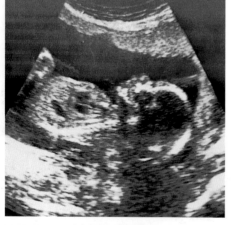

TAKING A LOOK WITH SOUND
The previously hidden world of the womb is made visible through ultrasound. By using ultrasonic waves, it is possible to form images of a foetus growing inside its mother's womb. Ultrasound is also used to examine internal organs.

There are millions of cells in a single drop of blood

LOOKING CLOSER

For centuries, microscopes have permitted scientists to look at minute particles invisible to the naked eye. Today, microbiologists use powerful electron microscopes to study cells, enabling them to gain a better understanding of the essential processes of life. This highly magnified image of a blood sample was created using a scanning electron microscope. It shows three common blood cells – red (erythrocytes), white (lymphocytes), and blue (platelets).

THE CODE OF LIFE

Deoxyribonucleic acid (DNA) holds the very code of life itself. It is found in the nucleus of every cell and carries genetic information about an individual. The structure of DNA consists of two slender spiral strands that twist around each other to form a shape called a double helix. The strands are held together by atoms known as bases. Scientists around the world are now working together to map the entire sequence of human DNA.

UNIQUE FINGERPRINTS

In 1984, DNA was recognized internationally as a legal means of identification. Within a single DNA molecule is a sequence of information that is unique to an individual, apart from identical twins. Forensic scientists are able to identify a chemical sequence (above) to determine whether DNA samples are from the same person. The sequence can be taken from a tiny amount of evidence such as a single strand of hair, or a drop of blood discovered at the scene of a crime.

White blood cells do not attack nanorobots as they are made from a neutral material

NANOROBOTS

The notion of engineering on a minuscule scale was first discussed in the late 1950s. Today, it is becoming a reality. Using high-powered electron microscopes, scientists can examine and manipulate things at an atomic level. They are developing nanorobots – micro-machines that will be small enough to travel through the bloodstream. They will repair or remove diseased tissue at a molecular level. The nanorobots shown in this illustration are destroying diseased tissue inside a human blood vessel.

Nanorobot's spinning blades destroy a tumour

Nanorobot attacks a blood clot

Image is stored in computer

Bases are joined together in complementary pairs

Sequence of bases makes up the cell's genetic code

Several thousand base pairs make up a gene

INSTANT INFORMATION

Using a digital camera, a doctor takes a photograph of a patient's eye for his medical records. The image can then be displayed on a computer screen, and stored for future reference. Soon, computerized medical records will be drawn up for every individual. Patients attending the doctor's surgery or hospital appointment will have their medical records immediately available. Eventually, a patient's entire medical history, along with his or her genetic code, will be carried everywhere by the patient, stored on a smart card (pp. 58–59).

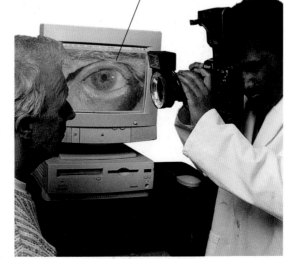

Model of a DNA double helix

Genetic engineering

ONE OF THE MOST SIGNIFICANT legacies of the 20th century will be the development of our ability to manipulate life through genetic engineering. The human race is poised on the edge of a future that may be able to make fundamental changes to the living organisms that share our planet. What would normally take millions of years to develop through the process of natural selection may soon be achieved in a laboratory overnight. One day, geneticists may be able to remove traits from human beings that society considers undesirable for social or health reasons. They could then replace them with more acceptable characteristics. But the results of this kind of genetic engineering will not only change human biology – they will alter society itself.

MONSTER MYTH
Some people fear that interfering with genetic science will produce new monsters like the Chimera of ancient mythology, which is part lion, part goat, and part snake.

PEST CONTROL
By genetically modifying a virus with a toxin taken from a north African scorpion, it is possible to produce a much more effective control for one particular pest, the cabbage looper. The modified virus improves the speed of the looper's destruction by 25 per cent.

CHEMICAL CODES
The DNA molecule is composed of units called nucleotides that form complicated sequences. Enzymes are able to cut sequences to change something genetically. Understanding how an enzyme works allows us to manipulate the genes.

Patient with cystic fibrosis relies on medical treatment to survive

Harvard mouse specially engineered for cancer research

GENETIC THERAPY
Congenital disorders happen when a defective gene is passed on from parents to their children. These disorders have a devastating effect on a family and can result in a lifelong dependence on medical treatment. Genetic engineering offers some hope for the future. Geneticists can now isolate the genes that carry diseases such as cystic fibrosis and muscular dystrophy. It is hoped that it will soon be possible to replace the defective genes with healthy ones.

ONE OF A KIND
Genetic engineering may result in research or business organizations owning their own life forms. This mouse, genetically engineered for cancer research at Harvard University, was the world's first mammal to be patented in 1988. Some geneticists argue that if they create a unique living organism they should have rights over its use. However, an international ethical debate has stalled further patents.

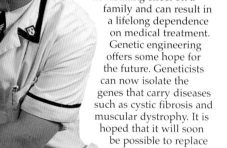

Cloning animals and plants

One of the most incredible, yet troubling, developments of genetic science is the ability to clone animals and plants. A clone is an exact genetic copy of the DNA donor. In 1997, the world was introduced to Dolly the sheep, the first mammal to be cloned from a cell of another adult. Geneticists have already cloned human embryos for medical research. If their techniques are perfected it may soon be possible to clone human organs and tissue for transplant. However, many people have concerns about cloning whole human beings.

Sheep providing cell

Sheep to be cloned

DNA of sheep to be cloned

DNA taken from cell

Snipped DNA

DNA is fused with cell

New DNA

Cloned embryo is implanted in third sheep

Sterile soil substitute is full of nutrients

Dolly, the identical copy of DNA donor

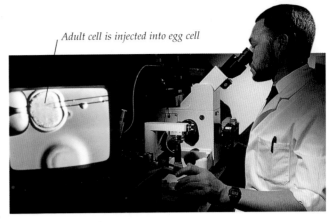

Adult cell is injected into egg cell

SPARK OF LIFE
There are a number of ways of transferring DNA from one cell to another. In Dolly's case, a cell was injected into an egg that had its nucleus removed (above). A spark of electricity fused the cells and promoted growth. Other methods for transferring include using bacteria as a carrier or firing tiny gene-carrying particles into the cell.

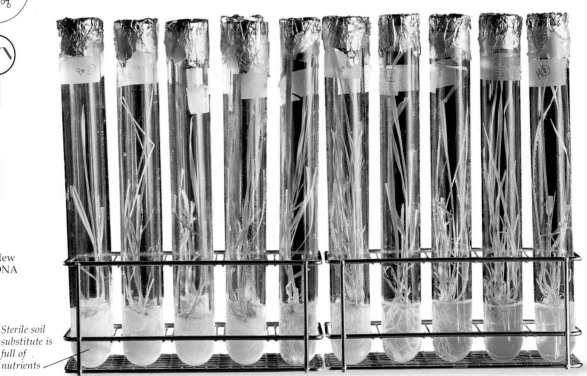

THE BIRTH OF DOLLY
The process for creating Dolly involved three sheep. A cell was taken from the first ewe and its genes were removed. DNA was then taken from a cell of a second ewe and fused with the first cell. Once the embryo was developed, it was implanted into a third sheep, to be carried there until Dolly was born.

Dolly the sheep

PLANT REVOLUTION
In the plant kingdom there are several methods of transferring DNA, such as using bacteria as a carrier or firing tiny particles carrying genes into the cell. Genetic modification has been employed in farming to increase crop yields, improve pest resistance, or boost a crop's ability to thrive in a hostile environment. These cereal plants (above) are clones grown from the single cell of a genetically modified plant.

COUNTLESS CLONES
Cattle have been successfully cloned in the United States permitting the mass reproduction of unlimited numbers of identical cows. Cloning cattle would enable farmers to maximize the benefits of desirable traits, such as high milk yields and tender meat. Cows are also being genetically engineered to produce special proteins in their milk for people with specific dietary needs.

Future foods?

THE WORLD DEMAND for food increases daily as the population grows. But drought and crop failures have not been eliminated, and pests have become increasingly resistant to insecticides. Meanwhile, sophisticated consumers are demanding year-round fresh food, but they are also concerned about the possible side effects of the chemicals used to increase crop yields. By changing the DNA of plants and animals, scientists hope to revolutionize agriculture. Although there are substantial benefits, the genetic engineering of food remains controversial. Some scientists are concerned that, if they manipulate nature, it may be impossible to reverse mistakes.

FAST FOOD IN SPACE
There is endless fascination with the kind of food that space travellers eat. In the 1960s, astronauts survived on a diet of dehydrated food and tablets that contained nutritional supplements. Although convenient to carry into space, all the pleasure of eating was lost.

FUTURE FOOD IN SPACE
If one day we choose to live in space, it will be essential to grow food there. This artist's impression of a farming spaceship, shaped like a giant wheel, demonstrates how crops could be grown on a space station. Centrifugal force substitutes for gravity, and the growing crops release oxygen, replenishing the ship's supply.

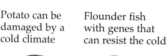

Potato can be damaged by a cold climate

Flounder fish with genes that can resist the cold

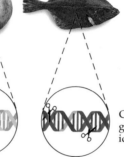

DNA of potato

Cold resistant gene is cut out

Cold resistant gene is identified

SWEET TOOTH
Those of us who find it hard to resist a slice of chocolate cake may in the future be able to eat as much as we like. Tomorrow's treats will be genetically engineered to be less fattening, so we can literally have our cake and eat it.

Peanuts often cause a fatal allergic reaction

ALLERGY-FREE NUTS
Most food allergies are slight, and result in no more than a mild rash or stomach ache. But some reactions are very severe. The allergic reaction to peanuts, for example, can be particularly serious, causing severe illness or even death. Research is now underway to manipulate the genes of nuts so that in the future all risk of allergic reaction is removed.

FUTURE PEST CONTROL
In recent years, large amounts of chemical fertilizers, herbicides, and pesticides have been used to protect plants and encourage growth. By genetically modifying crops to be pest resistant and hardy, it may be possible to eliminate the need for crop spraying.

FISH 'N' CHIPS
A gene from a flounder fish (above right) could be transferred to a potato to make it frost resistant. The potato could be grown in cold conditions, benefiting societies living in hostile climates. But people are worried about the long-term effects of exchanging genes between species that could never naturally interbreed.

Gene modification is by one of the following methods:
• gene gun
• through bacteria
• bursts of electricity or chemicals
• injection

Cold resistant gene incorporated into potato's DNA

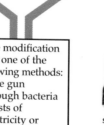

Genetically modified DNA produces a frost-resistant potato

ACCELERATED GROWTH
After being genetically modified to produce a growth hormone, this fish is large enough for eating after just 18 months instead of the usual three years. Genetic modification could be the answer to depleting fish stocks. But along with similar experiments on other animals, it raises many serious ethical questions.

A BETTER DEAL FOR ALL?
The shelves in supermarkets may soon be filled with genetically modified fruit and vegetables. Fruit and vegetables can be made to taste better and even be more nutritious. They will be longer-lasting so there will be far less wastage, which will make them more plentiful and cheaper to buy. Genes that have a negative effect on a certain type of food can be removed and replaced with a beneficial one. And certain fruits and vegetables could also be genetically engineered to defend themselves against harmful viruses, fungi, and insects so they will no longer need to be sprayed with chemical fertilizers.

Strawberries can be modified to be sweeter and juicier

Tomatoes can be modified to withstand common pests, improving their yield by 20 to 30 per cent

Sweetcorn can be modified to resist the corn borer pest, which destroys 20 per cent of maize in Europe

Soft fruits such as pears and kiwi fruit can be modified to have a longer shelf life in the shops

Bananas can be modified to produce a range of vaccines

Exotic fruits such as the pineapple can be modified to grow in colder climates

Cauliflowers can be modified to be red or blue to appeal more to children

Potatoes can be modified to hold less water so that, when cooked as chips, they will absorb less oil

Cabbages and broccoli can be modified to grow with higher concentrations of health-giving chemicals

39

Changing bodies

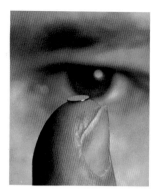

OUR BODIES ARE fragile and complex, they are vulnerable to disease, and are easily damaged. In recent years, medical advances, along with the development of new drugs and materials, have allowed surgeons to replace body parts that are damaged, diseased, or simply worn out. Successful organ transplants mean that people can now survive diseases that twenty years ago would have killed them. Prosthetics (artificial parts) are being developed that give the person wearing them high levels of control, comfort, reliability, and agility. Scientists are also experimenting with implants to combine human cells and microchips, creating physical links between the human body and the latest computer technology. The potential for this work is enormous. One day, implanted machines and computers may mean that the human body will function more efficiently and last longer.

Polyethene (PE) finger joints for arthritis

Titanium and polyethene elbow

BODY CHIPS
Scientists are developing a method of connecting human nerve cells to a silicon chip. This could counter the effects of brain damage. Already, some forms of blindness have been overcome using semiconductor retinal implants to stimulate the optic nerve.

Anti epilepsy unit

Pacemaker can download information

Mother-of-pearl from an oyster shell

FUTURE TRANSPLANTS
Organ transplants are a regular procedure, even among young children. This baby (right) became the youngest person in the world to receive an organ transplant when she was only five days old. Scientists are experimenting with genetically modified animal organs to overcome donor shortages.

REGENERATING BONES
Instead of replacing a damaged limb with a prosthetic, human bone can now be regenerated using mother-of-pearl shell mixed with bone or blood cells (left). When implanted, it stimulates the growth of new bone.

Electronic pain relief

Silicon chip controls the mind

Cyborgs are part human, part machine

Skin is grown in fibrin gel

NEW SKIN
New skin can be made artificially by placing skin cells in a nutrient-rich gel. Fragments of replicating skin cells multiply rapidly – it takes only three weeks to grow into 1 sq. m (11 sq. ft) of new skin. The artificial skin is used on patients who need skin grafts, perhaps as the result of a fire.

Titanium and polyethene implant to mobilize the toe joint

WIRED MAN
Fictional cyborgs, such as Captain Picard from *Star Trek* (right), with their enhanced strength and superhuman sensory organs may soon become a reality. In the future, the boundaries between humans and machines will become blurred, with the creation of real cyborgs, like the "Wired Man" (above).

Artificial eye

Silicone rubber to replace external ear

Silicone rubber to replace damaged nose

Artificial larynx allowing speech

Polymethylmethacrylate (PMMA) used for gums and teeth

Artificial eye

Hard-wearing ceramic coated shoulder joint

HELPING TO HEAR
Some forms of deafness can be helped by using electronics. Implants are attached to the bone behind the ear. Electrodes from the implant reach the cochlea, the part of the inner ear that allows us to hear. Impulses then travel in the normal way through the nerve pathways, sending signals to the brain, which interprets them as sound.

Titanium nails hold fractured bones together

Cardiac pacemaker to regulate heartbeat

Bone staples pull the bone together as they warm up

Hand cover

Aortic valve made from PMMA

Aortic valve made from polytetrafluoroethene (PTFE)

Titanium device to fuse two vertebrae together

Stainless steel cylinder to unblock artery

ELECTRONICALLY ABLE
In the past, prosthetics were made from metal or simply carved out of wood. They were uncomfortable and awkward to use. Today, most artificial limbs use electronic circuits. This arm is operated by tensing the stump muscles in what remains of the limb. This produces tiny electrical signals that are detected and amplified by sensors. In the future, an electronic motor could be controlled by nerve signals from the stump.

Cover to battery compartment

Hand cover

Artificial cobalt chromium hip with ceramic head

Prosthetic cover

Hip replacement in titanium with a chrome head and polyethene cup is light and flexible

Wearer can take part in everyday activities

Stainless steel cylinder to unblock large blood vessels

Flexible polyesther tubes bypass damaged veins

REVOLUTIONARY LEG
This artificial limb has a built-in knee socket. The socket contains a computer chip and pneumatic cylinders. These allow the wearer to walk without having to concentrate on each step. The limb is so advanced and flexible that the wearer can enjoy all kinds of physical activity such as jogging and cycling.

Polyethene and cobalt alloy provide smooth movement in this artificial knee joint

THE BIONIC HUMAN BEING
All the prosthetics or other additions visible in this resin body have been used because they are made from lightweight, flexible, and long-lasting materials. They are used to replace many different parts of the body that may have been damaged by disease, a traumatic accident, or old age. Ceramic combined with cobalt chromium replaces the worn-out, brittle joints of the elderly, and broken bones can be held in place by pins while natural healing takes place. When blood vessels become blocked or lose their elasticity, they can be bypassed. And damaged soft tissue can be replaced by latex. Scientists are constantly finding a new medical use for the most unlikely materials.

Bone plates made from carbon fibre encourage bone growth

Pneumatic cylinders allow natural walking at different speeds

Titanium and polyethene make a strong and wear-resistant ankle

Running shoe fits securely on artificial limb

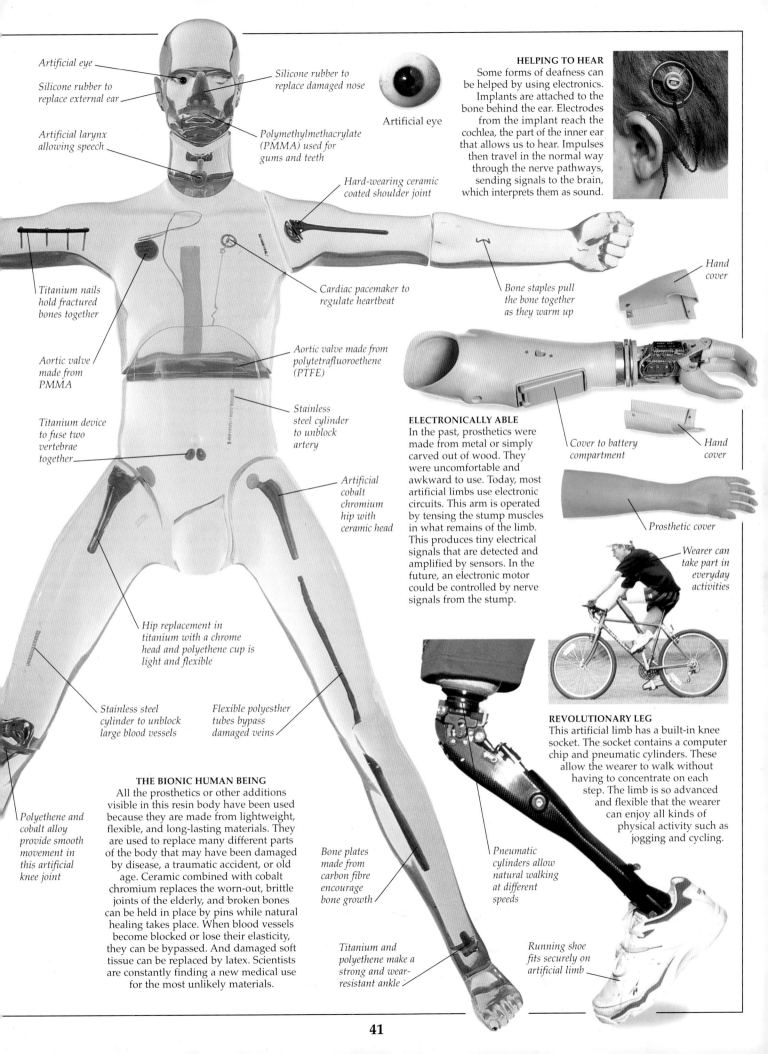

Robots and robotics

Humanoid shape considered more "friendly"

SINCE THE FIRST AUTOMATED production lines were put into operation in the 1950s, it has been obvious that many routine jobs can be carried out effectively by mechanical means. Robots free people from difficult or dangerous tasks such as bomb disposal or welding. And it often costs an employer less to maintain a robot than to employ a person, so their use reduces jobs in the workplace. Today's advanced robots are mobile, and equipped with television cameras for sight and electronic sensors for touch. Recent developments include robots that can walk, balance themselves if they start to fall, and recognize faces and gestures. Some organizations have been researching robotics for several years with the aim of seeing how technology can be applied to practical use in the home. It is possible that, by the year 2011, a mechanical housekeeper will cook our meals and do all the chores.

MANNY THE ROBOT
Robot builders have moved on from industrial machines to build robots that look and move something like people. These robots vary in design and size, but there are already several that are humanoid. This one, nicknamed Manny, was developed to test protective clothing such as spacesuits, fire-fighting gear, and clothing worn in hazardous environments, for example when dealing with chemicals.

Joints are fully articulated

Ability to balance delicate objects

System set up to simulate sweating and breathing

SLAVES IN THE FIELDS
Mechanical workers have long been thought of as a means of escaping from the drudgery of repetitive or unpleasant work. This illustration from a 1896 edition of *La Science Illustrée* shows robot farm-workers of the future. Fortunately, our countryside is not littered with mechanical fish, but robots are becoming a much more familiar feature in today's industrial society, and farms are certainly more mechanized.

The Czech word "robot" originally referred to slave-like workers in the field

AUTOMATION IN INDUSTRY
Robots do not get bored! They can do all sorts of repetitive tasks with accuracy and consistency. Industrial computer-controlled robots are used in car production to carry out a variety of tasks such as welding, drilling, and the paint-spraying of body parts. A robot is programmed to carry out a particular task, such as welding a car door, while a computer tracks its movements. Afterwards, the computer takes over completely, instructing the robot to move in exactly the same pattern over and over again.

ROBOTS IN SPACE

A Remote Manipulator System (RMS) arm was developed for use by US astronauts in space. It is seen here (left) moving some equipment from the space shuttle *Endeavour* when the astronauts were servicing the Hubble Space Telescope in 1993.

RMS arm was extended from cargo bay door of shuttle

US astronaut on RMS arm

Sports robot is programmed to respond to partner

Sensors in hands detect the ball

Can use sensors in its arms to shake hands with people

BALL PARTNER

A Japanese electronics company has developed a robot that can play handball. It does this by reacting to voice commands, identifying colours, and even detecting human faces. The makers plan to develop robots that will serve the human population in the 21st century. Although this particular robot is only programmed to play handball, it is hoped that later models will be able to work in factories, hospitals, or in the home.

Robot contains the latest microchip technology

Hinged joints permit robot to walk on uneven surfaces

Video camera

Foot contains sensors

ATTILA, THE ROBOT INSECT

This insect robot has 23 motors and 150 sensors that allow it to move across inhospitable terrain by itself. Its ability to perform simple tasks may make it useful for on-the-spot repairs inside machinery.

BOMB DISPOSAL UNIT

This radio-controlled bomb disposal robot is removing a suspect briefcase from a car. The robot is controlled by an operator who can "see" its movements from a safe distance by using the onboard video camera.

Fire extinguishers operate if bomb explodes

Internal battery lasts 15 minutes

CLIMBING ROBOT

This humanoid robot is capable of deciding how to move across a variety of terrain, climb stairs, and recover its balance if pushed. The robot, dubbed "Honda-sapiens" by its creators, is able to decide for itself when to step over an obstacle, and when to find an alternative route. The robot is 2 m (6 ft) tall and weighs 210 kg (463 lb).

Stays upright when walking up a slope

Honda-sapiens is the first robot in the world that can climb stairs

Machines that think

ARTIFICIAL INTELLIGENCE TAKES OVER
The science fiction film *2001: A Space Odyssey*, based on the book by Arthur C. Clarke (b.1917), is a story ahead of its time. Today's supercomputers do not yet have the powers of the mad computer HAL, which controls the Jupiter-bound spaceship in the film, but it is possible that they will in the future.

MANY PEOPLE BELIEVE that by the middle of the 21st century the world will be populated by "smart" robots, which will be able to make their own judgments and decisions. These robots will be intelligent, independent, and able to communicate with each other. They will specialize in specific functions, so a robot that can travel at great speeds will not also play championship chess. However, their skills, overall range of knowledge, and ability to intercommunicate will provide them with great power. Science fiction writer Isaac Asimov (1920-92) once wrote "a robot may not injure a human being, or through inaction allow a human being to come to harm." Some scientists now predict that robots will become so advanced that they will be able to make up their own minds. Robots may one day offer us a life free from drudgery, but such a future is not without risk.

Kasparov ponders his next move

Supercomputer Deeper Blue

IN TROUBLE WITH DEEPER BLUE
In 1997, IBM chess supercomputer Deeper Blue beat grandmaster Gary Kasparov in a six-game chess match for the first time. Kasparov had played a less sophisticated version of the machine before and won, but in Kasparov's own words, this time the computer "suddenly played like a god". Deeper Blue may be capable of analyzing 200 million moves per second and seeing 20 moves ahead, but it cannot run any other software or perform other tasks while playing.

Special sensors check for smoke and humidity

ROBOT WATCH
The Cybermotion SR2 is a security robot used by the Los Angeles County Museum in the USA to detect intruders, or hazards such as gas, fire, or steam. SR2 navigates the museum without cables or tracks, using a built-in electronic map. It uses sonar to avoid bumping into any of the valuable exhibits, and communicates with a central computer by radio.

Radio link enables Elma to communicate with computer

ELMA, A ROBOT WITH INSTINCT
Robots ruled by intelligence rather than instructions are being designed by roboticists. Elma, an insect robot built by the Department of Cybernetics at Reading University in the UK, was constructed solely to learn how to walk. Elma has six independent legs, each of which is operated by an individual motor. Elma was pre-programmed by her creators to try out different leg movements. The aim of the experiment was to see if she could move over a surface without falling over by coordinating each of her leg movements independently (pp. 46-47).

Central processing brain organizes body-balancing operation

Contact sensors in aluminium leg allow Elma to feel when she is actually touching the surface .

Elma at rest

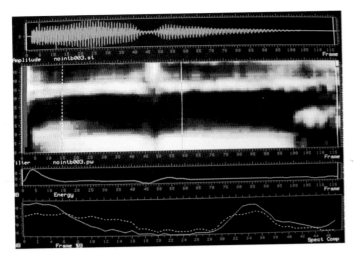

VOICE RECOGNITION

Computer interfaces still rely heavily on the keyboard and the mouse. This is set to change, as scientists have already begun work on new systems that will allow computers to recognize human voice patterns and understand verbal instructions. The computer graphics seen here image the speech synthesized word "baby".

ROBOT SERVANTS?

A friendly machine doing all the household chores is a popular but unlikely vision of robots in the future. We are a long way from having the technology to create a multi-functional robot with the ability to carry out household duties. Even the simple task of making a cup of tea and delivering it to you in bed is beyond the capability of current robototics.

Sensors detect how much force to apply when gripping an object

Artificial tendons generate electrical signals

Robot can grip a variety of objects

APPLYING PRESSURE WITH THE LIGHTEST OF TOUCHES

The human hand is extremely complicated so it is very difficult to design a machine that can imitate its complex movements. This electrically operated four-fingered robotic hand was designed to investigate force control. The rubber fingertips contain tiny pressure sensors, which can detect how much force is required to grip an object. Information from the sensors is fed to a microprocessor, which is intelligent enough to control the action of all four fingers at once. Instead of muscles and tendons, each finger is operated by wires. Like Elma, the hand can learn from its mistakes, but has no residual memory. Once it is switched off all that it has learned will be forgotten.

Elma takes a tumble

Elma regains her balance

Legs awkwardly positioned

Continued on next page

Artificial intelligence

Scientists and engineers all around the world are trying to build "smart" robots – that is robots capable of learning. At Reading University, UK, robots that can learn how to perform simple functions have been developed. Elma can learn to walk, and a group of wheeled robots known as the Seven Dwarfs are capable of recognizing objects and making decisions about how to move based on this information. The future for robots now lies in their being able to learn from their experiences and pass information on to other robots.

Infrared transmitters send out signals to other Dwarfs

1 COMING TOGETHER
When a group of Dwarfs are put together they transmit a "Here I am" signals while also listening for other robots. If a robot hears a number of these signals grouped together it will move towards them.

Ribbon cable connects sensors to the motors in the base of the Dwarf

Ultrasonic sensors stop Dwarf from bumping into objects

Metal bumper in case of collision

THE SEVEN DWARFS
The Seven Dwarfs are a collection of identical robots programmed to do the same thing. Eventually the roboticists who designed them hope to give the machines their own individual characteristics and design a superior communications system, which would allow them to pass on more complex information.

Motor-driven wheels can go forwards or backwards at varying speeds

Fully rechargeable onboard battery can last up to six hours

Each leg motor is matched to another inside Elma's body

Elma's glass fibre body is similar to the chitinous exoskeleton of a real insect

Elma learns quickly how to recover from a nose dive

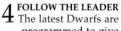

2 IN COMMUNICATION
The Dwarfs learn to avoid bumping into things, including each other. But they are also programmed to flock towards each other. They can communicate efficiently by transmitting and receiving infrared signals.

3 GETTING TOGETHER?
The Dwarfs move about flocking and avoiding each other. When one finds itself with a clear, open space ahead of it, it is programmed to transmit a signal that says "Follow me". The other three Dwarfs are programmed to follow and turn to do so.

Dwarfs learn how to control their wheels to avoid hitting each other and other objects

Future operators will be able to control truck from anywhere

Computer operator monitors progress of Navlab

Each Dwarf transmits its own unique frequency

Navlab can travel at speeds of up to 60 km/h (37 mph)

NAVLAB II
The Navlab II is a self-driving truck. It is controlled by a computer called ALVINN (Autonomous Land Vehicle in a Neural Network). The computer is "taught" how to drive by a human instructor. Through video cameras and a laser range finder, ALVINN can monitor the road and recognize markings and junctions. Another computer called EDDIE (Efficient Decentralized Database and Interface Experiment) provides additional collision avoidance software.

4 FOLLOW THE LEADER
The latest Dwarfs are programmed to give preference to a leader signal over a group one. Sometimes more than one leader signal is transmitted at a time, and the group will split, with individual Dwarfs following the nearest signal. When a leader reaches another group, it reverts to using the "Here I am" signal.

THE FUTURE FOR ROBOTS LIKE ELMA
It is hoped that having learned how to walk, Elma and robots like her will be able to cope with a variety of different surfaces. Elma has been given a radio link that allows her to communicate directly with a computer. In this way she can send and receive information about her environment. This information can be used by the computer to produce a 3-D mapped picture. In the future, a computer will not be needed because it will be possible for robots like Elma to be entirely self-sufficient.

Dwarfs are also self-aware

Virtual reality

SEEING THE WORLD THROUGH TWO-COLOUR GLASSES
Before virtual reality, there was three-dimensional cinema. In the 1950s, members of the 3-D movie audience were each given a pair of cardboard glasses. These were essential – without them the film would be unfocussed. Film-makers designed shots to impress the audience by directing the action towards them. People would duck as objects seemed to fly out of the screen!

Glasses had lenses of different colours

THE EDGES BETWEEN reality and virtual reality are becoming blurred. It is already possible to virtually "experience" an exciting activity such as skiing down a mountain. As computers become more powerful, the virtual experience will become even more real. You will feel the wind in your hair, the frost on your eyebrows, the gentle heat of the sun on your face, as well as the shudder through your ski boots as you speed down the mountain. Virtual reality also has practical uses. It provides us with very beneficial medical applications. Not only can it be used to teach surgical techniques, surgeons are already able to carry out procedures with it, using robotic arms. Imagine the benefits of a surgeon in Australia being able to perform an operation on a patient in Mexico! In the future, virtual reality will be used to train people in many activities, from truck drivers and engineers to mountain climbers and atomic physicists.

REALITY CENTRE
Virtual reality is an effective design tool. It allows manufacturers to model products with a computer instead of having to build expensive prototypes. The people in this picture are viewing a virtual oil rig. A bank of powerful computers, performing a billion operations per second, allows them to be guided through a three-dimensional virtual space to view the oil rig from any angle. The wrap-around screen and quadrophonic sound effects give a spectacular effect.

"Flychair" has controls that allow the person sitting in it to decide how to "travel" around the oil rig

It is possible to examine complicated machinery in great detail

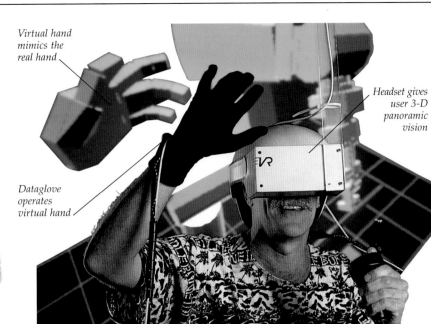

Virtual hand mimics the real hand

Headset gives user 3-D panoramic vision

Dataglove operates virtual hand

VIRTUAL ENTERTAINMENT

As yet, virtual reality has not been fully developed for use in the home. Instead, people have "virtual rides" in entertainment centres, watching surfers riding the waves in remarkable and nerve-wracking three-dimensional reality. In the 21st century, this will all change, with virtual reality machines in the home (pp. 28-29), and special virtual sensory suits that will allow you to experience the ride itself.

VIRTUAL CONTROL

This visor and glove allow the viewer to interact with a virtual experience. The glove on his hand provides feeling, allowing him the sensation of touch. He is programming a virtual reality system that will be used to control a real robot sent into dangerous situations, such as the ocean floor or a reactor core in a nuclear power station.

Touch-sensitive virtual pages can be "turned" by readers

VIRTUAL BOOK

Many precious books cannot be handled by the public because they may get damaged. To solve this problem, computer experts are developing virtual books. The original book is photographed and scanned. A special software programme imitates the feel and structure of the book and readers are provided with an opportunity to "virtually" turn the pages, just as they would leaf through an ordinary book.

Virtual image on screen shows surgeon where to operate

SURGICAL ARM

Surgeons are already using virtual reality to assist them in operations. Virtual reality programmes can be used by trainees to develop their skills. Even experienced surgeons sometimes need to practise a difficult procedure before carrying it out on the patient. This robot can be used by a brain surgeon to pinpoint diseased areas of the brain such as tumours.

Crescent-shaped screen fills the horizontal view of the participants, immersing them completely

Robotic arm inside a human skull

Seeing the invisible

X-RAY SPECS
Children had fun with these pretend X-ray specs, launched in the 1950s. They could use their imagination to pretend they were spies or special agents, capable of seeing through the walls of secret buildings, or even through skin to their own skeleton. If, one day in the future, X-ray specs do become a reality, they would certainly be used by everyone.

WITH THE NAKED EYE we can see the world around us, and with a little assistance we can see it more clearly. Spectacles help those with poor sight, microscopes allow us to see minute detail, and telescopes permit us to see far out into the distance. But there are still many things that remain invisible to us. Visible light is just one small area in a huge electromagnetic spectrum that moves from gamma and cosmic rays through X-rays, ultraviolet radiation, infrared, and microwave, to radio waves. Each of these parts of the spectrum allow us to see the world, and the Universe, in slightly different ways. Some are familiar, but others are just being discovered. X-rays have been used in medicine for more than a century. Radar was first used in World War II to locate enemy aircraft and ships. Today, ultraviolet light can be used to help drivers to see better at night, while space telescopes are sending back incredible images from deepest space.

View of road ahead with ordinary headlights

View of road ahead with ultraviolet headlights

Ultraviolet headlights

Solar panels

Antenna relays data back to Earth via radio

VISION ON
It is hardly surprising that most road accidents occur at night. In poor visibility, a driver has far less warning of a hazard ahead, and therefore less time to avoid it. Brighter headlights are not practical because they dazzle oncoming traffic. But ultraviolet light, invisible to the human eye, can be used. It reflects off fluorescent material, warning the driver to stop in time.

Contents of lorry visible on screen

OUT IN SPACE
We can now look out into space and see the birth of stars. The Hubble Space Telescope was launched in 1990 to look at the optical and ultraviolet Universe. In 1995, it sent back the first high-quality images of the Eagle Nebula (left), a huge cloud of gas and dust, which is 7,000 light years from our planet.

Columns of hydrogen gas act as incubators for new stars

SECURITY CHECK
Customs officials at airports and ports throughout the world use X-ray machines to check the contents of luggage. With new technology, larger and more sophisticated machines have been designed that are capable of checking the entire contents of vehicles, such as this lorry (right). Previously it could take anything up to 24 hours to carry out a security check – now it can be done in a matter of minutes.

VIEW FROM SPACE

This colour-enhanced image of an earthquake was taken by the ERS-1 satellite in space. It is the first view of an earthquake from space and shows how the ground was displaced in the US state of California in 1992. The closer the colour bands are, the greater the ground displacement.

Coloured bands show shockwaves of earthquake

Pilot's cabin

OCEAN FLOOR

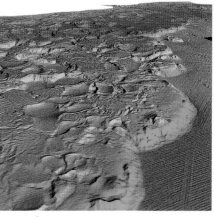

This sonar image taken of the sea bed in the Gulf of Mexico was made by ships recording sound echoes from the ocean floor. The different colours show the various depths. Buried rock sediment, deposited from the Mississippi River, creates a crater landscape that resembles the surface of the Moon.

Infrared goggles gives soldier ability to see in the dark

STEALTH FIGHTER

It is difficult to make something as large as an aeroplane disappear, but that is what Lockheed attempted to do with their F-117 Stealth Fighter. Its angular shape deflects radar beams, making it difficult to spot and almost impossible for guided missiles to attack. Although the fighter can be cloaked from radar, it is not invisible to other detection devices, such as thermal imaging.

TOMORROW'S KILLING MACHINE

Camouflage has been used to help soldiers and their weaponry blend into the background. However, the use of radar, ultra-sensitive listening devices, and thermal imaging makes it increasingly difficult for soldiers to "disappear". Military scientists are developing new cloaking devices so that soldiers and their equipment can hide from the enemy.

Security officials can see through 28 cm (11 in) of steel, revealing any secret cargo

Angular shape deflects radar beams

Head-up-display (HUD) projects tactical information into eyepiece

"Smart" weapons include a laser to pick out targets for guided weapons

Getting smaller

THE INVENTION OF THE TRANSISTOR in 1947, and its successor the integrated circuit in 1959, have transformed our world. Previously, cumbersome electron tubes in radios and television sets generated a lot of heat and had to be housed in large containers. Today, thousands of electrical components are etched onto tiny wafers of silicon to make microprocessors. This technology has spawned a computer industry that only a few years ago was unimaginable, with powerful hand-held computers that can be linked to satellites to provide e-mail and Internet access. In the past, a radio smaller than a mouse seemed unimaginable, but now one exists. In the future, components will get even smaller still.

IN MINIATURE
The integrated circuit is an essential feature of modern technology. It replaced the diverse separate components of early electronics. Many thousands of individual transistors can be carried on a tiny chip of silicon, changing the look and the way electronics can be applied.

ENIAC had to be re-wired each time it was programmed

MONSTER MACHINE
Before the introduction of transistors and integrated circuits, scientists relied upon valve technology for their electronic computers. This meant that computers were extremely large and not very powerful. One of the first computers, ENIAC, weighed 30 tonnes and occupied a whole room.

COMPACT EARPHONES
Compact, portable cassette machines became widely available in the 1980s. Their high-quality sound was played back through small headphones. These have since been replaced by even smaller earpieces that fit right inside the ear.

POWER SUPPLY
These tiny, lightweight batteries can be used to power a whole range of electronic equipment, from watches to cameras.

RECORDING IN MINIATURE
The latest compact discs (above) can store sound, graphics, and moving images. Although they are small, they have a large memory. Now you can also record your own music on the tiniest of cassettes (left), with a quality of sound that is ten times better than when cassettes were invented in the 1970s.

PALMTOP COMPUTER
In less than 50 years computers have reduced in size so that now they can fit into the palm of your hand. The Psion may be small, but it is extremely powerful. It contains a personal organizer, a database, and a word processor, and it is programmable. In a world of fast communication, it can also send and receive messages, access the Internet, and exchange e-mail – all as you walk along the road.

Modem connection

Fully functional keyboard

Back-up battery for data storage

Flash card can be reused

Panasonic

CF DIGITAL

Card Shot
DIGITAL STILL CAMERA NV-DCF1

CUTTING OUT THE MIDDLE MAN
The need for film processing may soon be a thing of the past. Digital cameras record images directly onto a flash card, which is downloaded onto a computer for viewing. The images are easy to store and edit on the computer, so if you do not like the photograph, you can change it!

AN EARFUL OF MUSIC
Portable radios first became popular in the early 1960s. Today, integrated circuits have improved both the quality and reception so much that the radio can be small enough to fit right inside your ear.

Antenna needed for reception

Volume control

SCAN

RESET

Earpad

POCKET-SIZED TELEVISIONS
In the early days of television, all the working components were housed in a large, cumbersome wooden box. Today, integrated circuits allow us to package a television into a much smaller container. This television is small enough to fit inside a pocket.

Television can be watched almost anywhere

UHF 21 30 40 50 60 68 CH

StarTAC

StarTAC

MOTOROLA

ESSENTIAL COMMUNICATION
Early mobile telephones were impractical, cumbersome, and required heavy batteries. Today's slimline mobiles are increasingly popular, and small enough to be carried inside a shirt pocket. This Motorola StarTAC is one of the smallest in the world. To cater for the increase in demand for airspace, the human voice is digitized before it is transmitted.

OFFICE ON THE ARM
Future technology will allow people to work from any location. In the 21st century "offices on the arm", like this prototype, are likely to be a way of keeping in touch with business contacts from anywhere and at any time of the day. It will have a computer and mobile telephone, which can be connected to the Internet. It will be powered by mains, batteries, or by a special vest worn by the user, which will convert body heat into enough electricity to run the system. The benefits are obvious: working patterns will become more flexible and the problems of commuting will be reduced.

Fold away screen

Laboratories

BT

Alarm clock

4:37:18

H M AC C MRc

Touch pad controls

Mobile office houses a 2 gigabyte hard drive

Lighter than air

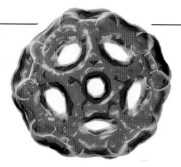

BUCKYBALLS
Buckyballs are tiny spherical structures made up of 60 carbon atoms. They may become the building blocks of a new kind of engineering, at a molecular level – creating nanomachines (pp. 34-35).

HEAT RESISTANT TILES IN SPACE
Silica tiles line the underside of the *Columbia* space shuttle. The heat-dissipating tiles are made from a high quality sand, and are used to protect the shuttle from the extreme temperatures as it re-enters the Earth's atmosphere.

NEW MATERIALS ARE being developed all the time. The invention of plastic in the early 20th century revolutionized our world, and became the lightweight alternative to traditional materials such as wood, metal, and glass. There are now hundreds of different types of plastic and others are being developed. Plastics are very adaptable and can be used to make anything from hard-wearing toys to pliable contact lenses. However, most plastics are not biodegradable, so millions of tonnes of waste plastic cannot be disposed of safely. New materials and processes may provide solutions, but in the meantime, scientists are developing more environmentally friendly materials for the next millennium. Some lightweight synthetics are stronger than steel, yet they can be woven into clothing. Foamed metals use less raw materials making them lighter whilst still retaining their strength.

Carbon cotton feels rougher than normal cotton

Pull a carbon thread as hard as you like – you cannot break it

LIGHTWEIGHT FRAME
Designed by Lotus Cars, this lightweight spaceframe chassis used in the Elise is a remarkable piece of engineering. It only weighs 68 kg (149 lbs) – half the usual steel equivalent, and can be easily lifted by two men. It is made from an aluminium alloy that is sensitive to heat. Instead of welding, the metal joints are held together by a powerful glue.

Rivets prevent joints coming apart

Bonded aluminium chassis is both lightweight and rigid

Lightweight steel subframe

Space age glue holds chassis parts together

The Lotus Elise

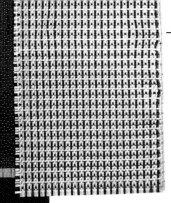

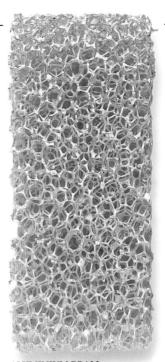

HIGH-TECH FIBRE
This material may look like cotton, but it is in fact carbon fibre. Unlike cotton, the thread of this lightweight fibre is almost impossible to break. It can be used in a whole range of products, from high-tech fighter planes to bicycle parts and golf clubs.

Frame is made of a fabric woven from carbon fibres

RIDE TO VICTORY
A racing bicycle must be light, strong, and aerodynamic. In 1992, a frame made from carbon fibre helped UK athlete Chris Boardman set a record of 54 km/h (34 mph) at the Barcelona Olympics.

IN THE HEAT OF THE MOMENT
Kevlar is a synthetic material similar to nylon, yet it is five times stronger than steel, more flexible than carbon fibre, and resistant to high temperatures. It can be woven into flak jackets to make them bullet-proof. The textile can stand temperatures as high as 400°C (752°F), making it much tougher than standard firefighting clothing.

Metal foams can be used in aeroplanes' body parts

ALUMINIUM FOAM
Scientists are taking ordinary metals, such as aluminium and zinc, and frothing them up to create amazing metal foams for all kinds of uses. Foamed metals are full of cavities so they use less material to fill the same space. They are strong, fireproof, and able to absorb sound. They already form parts of spacecraft, and will soon be used in aeroplanes. As they are lighter than ordinary metal they reduce fuel consumption.

SEAgel is water soluble at temperatures above 10°C (50°F)

SEAgel claims to be the first "lighter-than-air" solid

REVOLUTIONARY MATERIAL
Safe Emulsion Agar gel or SEAgel is an extremely lightweight solid – so light that it can balance on top of soap bubbles! It is produced from agar, which is derived from seaweed and is usually used as a thickening agent for food. Unlike plastic, SEAgel is biodegradable, soluble in water, and will not harm the environment. It could be used as an insulator, or to replace plastic as a packing material.

New frontiers

THROUGHOUT HISTORY, HUMANS have been driven to explore the far reaches of the globe in search of valuable minerals and new forms of life. Now that there are few areas of the world left unexplored, our sights have risen beyond our own planet and into space itself. Only a few centuries ago, powered by the wind, wooden ships travelled across the oceans into unchartered territories. In an echo of this recent history, we will in the future send spaceships powered by solar wind to explore space. We will colonize planets, and perhaps discover other forms of life. But we cannot rely on Earth to provide the materials to build and power these missions. Asteroids will be mined for resources and huge solar power satellites will be built to generate electricity. Only then can future colonies be established on the Moon and nearby planets.

FLY ME TO THE MOON
Holidays in space first captured people's imagination in the 1950s, when we were on the brink of sending the first human being into orbit. In the 21st century, there will be bases on the Moon, probably with lunar hotels in high demand!

Mining the asteroids

MINING THE UNIVERSE
The Moon and the asteroids are very rich in natural resources – minerals such as gold, platinum, nickel, and iron have already been identified. Moon dust contains hydrogen, which could be used to power rockets, as well as helium-3, a potential fuel for fusion reactors. One day, the Moon and the asteroids will be mined for raw materials, which will be used either for deeper space travel or sent back to Earth in huge solar-powered freighters. Asteroids might even be towed closer to the Earth, making it easier to exploit their enormous mineral wealth.

Structure moulded out of Mars rock

Mining the Moon

**H. G. Wells'
time machine**

**Photovoltaic
arrays collect
energy from the
Sun's rays**

**Space shuttle
docking**

TIME TRAVEL
Another area that has taxed our imaginations is time
travel. It is often a subject for works of fiction by
novelists such as H. G. Wells. Logically, if time travel
were to become a reality in the future, time travellers
would actually be visiting us right now!

**Colony is covered by a
transparent dome to
protect inhabitants from
the poisonous air**

**City can shelter
500 inhabitants**

INTERNATIONAL SPACE STATION
Space stations will provide astronauts with
a permanent base in Earth orbit for long periods of
time. The stations will act as laboratories for scientific
research into new materials and processes and also to
study the effects of long-term space flight. Work has
already begun on the International Space Station
(above), which is being jointly built and financed
by Russia, Japan, Europe, and the United States.

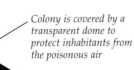

ANTIMATTER TRAVEL
For every particle that exists, there is a corresponding
anti-particle that is identical in every way except
for its opposite electrical charge. When matter and
antimatter meet, they annihilate each other, creating
energy. This artist's impression
shows a starship powered by
an antimatter rocket engine.
The idea is that matter and
antimatter would mix
and produce energy.

COLONY ON MARS
It only takes three days to reach the Moon, but
it would take six months to reach Mars. Because the planet is
so far away, it will be necessary to process fuel when the ship
reaches Mars for the return journey home. Giant protective
domes like this will need to be built to contain whole cities
of people in an a specially regulated atmosphere.

**City is built in a
crater on Pavonis
Mons, an extinct
volcano**

IS THERE ANYBODY OUT THERE?
The idea of aliens invading Earth has preoccupied
science fiction writers and film-makers. For many
years, people were convinced there was life on
Mars. Given the size of the Universe, the chances
of other life forms existing out there is high, but
whether they will look like humans, insects,
plants, or amoebas is
anybody's guess.

Living in the future

ALL AROUND US developments are taking place that will dramatically affect our lives. Molecular scientists are uncovering the fundamental processes of life itself. The inherited characteristics of our descendants may one day be in the hands of genetic engineers. If research into robotics is successful we may share our planet with intelligent machines. New materials are being developed all the time. Our future may not even be on this planet. Wherever it is, and whatever it is like, it is your future – find out about it, take part in it, enjoy it!

CITIES OF THE FUTURE
The dream of cities in space may soon become a reality. Ice discovered at the Moon's polar regions could be used to manufacture fuel and oxygen. This will provide the raw materials to build the first small space colonies.

GROWING POPULATION
Growth in the world's population increases demand on resources. International cooperation will be needed to ensure fair distribution and manage the environment.

Smart card microchip will carry information

UTOPIA National Identification Card
Cedula de Identidad

Name/Nombre
MARIA GONZALEZ
Sex/ Nationality/ Date of Birth/
Sexo Nacionalidad Fecha de Nacimiento
F UTO 12 JUL 57
Doc No/No de Doc Expires/Vencimiento
D23145890 12 JUL 97

Maria Gonzalez

ad West
N 55440

I<UTOD231458907<<<<<<<<<<<<<
3407127M9507122UTO<<<<<<<<<<8
MARIA<GONZALEZ<<<<<<<<<<<<<<<

"SMART" CARDS
Your full personal history could soon be recorded on a smart card. Combining driving licence, passport, medical records, financial status, qualifications, employment and criminal records, it will be used for all transactions.

MECHANICAL SERVANTS
Robots will require massive computing power if they are to assist us in all aspects of our everyday lives. We are likely to create machines more intelligent than ourselves, "smart" robots with the ability to make up their own minds.

VIRTUAL REALITY
Virtual reality is destined to make a significant impact on the way we live. We are now able to watch motor racing from the stand. In the future, we will be able to take "virtual" part in the race itself. Doctors will routinely use virtual reality to assist with their operations, while scientists, like this physicist, will use it to design experiments or work out theories.

NEW MATERIALS
New technology will alter our relationship with the physical world. Materials that can change shape could be used to make products less prone to damage. In building, materials could be instructed to change shape if, for example, the area was hit by an earthquake.

Glasses apparently crushed and unusable

Glasses "remember" their shape

DESIGNING LIFE
Molecular biology will play a significant role in the next century. The discovery of DNA and the development of genetic engineering means that we are able to manipulate life at a basic level. But this raises the question of how much we should interfere.

Receiver

Video postcard

COMMUNICATIONS
With Internet access and better technology, the world is getting smaller all the time. In the future, communications will include videophones and even "video postcards" (above).The cards will contain an extract of sounds and moving images. The captured moments and message would be activated by the receiver.

Liner can fly across the surface of the ocean

Video watch

TRANSPORT
Travel has played a major part in the history of the 20th century. Cars have given us freedom and independence, while aeroplanes make it possible to visit distant countries in the matter of a few hours. In the future bigger, faster, and more economic aeroplanes will be used to move people around, while satellite tracking systems will ensure safety is maintained in an increasingly crowded sky.

Double helix in a DNA molecule

ENGINEERING CROPS
Genetic engineering will allow us to manipulate crops making them insect resistant and capable of growing in harsh conditions. Genetic engineering could help provide enough food for the expanding world population, yet many scientists are deeply concerned about the consequences.

EXPLORING THE UNIVERSE
In the past, the difficulties of travelling seemed insurmountable, and gigantic ocean liners and aircraft were unimaginable. Yet, in the future, people will routinely leave Earth on spaceships to travel to other planets.

Artist's impression of Huygens spacecraft landing on Saturn's moon, Titan

Calendar of the future

Imagine travelling in a time machine into the middle of the 21st century – what do you think life would be like then? By examining current developments it is possible to make predictions about the future. Many of these predictions may happen and some may not, but those marked with asterisks could happen at any time.

2001	Common use of solar cells for residential power supply
2001	Wall-hung high-definition colour displays
2001	Electronic newspapers and paintings
2001	Hand videophone
2001	Home shopping
2001	Artificial blood and ears
2001	Full personal medical records stored on smart card
2004	Electronic notebook with contrast as good as paper
2005	Hydraulic chair for VR games
2005	Various forms of electronic addiction become a problem
2006	Tactile sensors comparable to human sensation
2007	Global electronic currency in use
2007	Determination of whole human DNA base sequence
2007	Robotized space vehicles and facilities
2009	Fire-fighting robots that can find and rescue people
2010	Smart clothes that can alter their thermal properties
2011	Multi-layer solar cells with efficiency greater than 50 per cent
2011	Robotic security and fire guards
2011	Housework robots to fetch, carry, clean, tidy, and organize
2014	Nanorobots roaming in blood vessels under own power
2014	Robotic pets
2014	Electronic shopping dominant
2014	First human landing on Mars
2020	3-D video-conferencing
2020	Genetic links of all diseases identified
2020	Artificial lungs, kidneys, and brain cells
2020	Cars that drive themselves on smart highways
2025	Deep underground cities in Japan
2025	New forms of plants and animals from genetic engineering
2025	Artificial liver
2025	Extension of lifespan to over 100
2025	Flying wing planes carry passengers at 960 km/h (600 mph)
2030	More robots than people in developed countries
2035	Fully functioning artificial eyes and legs
**	Collapse of the world's fisheries
**	Asteroid hits Earth
**	Long-term side effects of medication discovered
**	Viruses become immune to all known treatments
**	International financial collapse
**	Major information disruption
**	Nanotechnology takes off
**	Energy revolution
**	Collapse of the United Nations
**	Terrorism rises beyond the capability of government systems
**	First unambiguous contact with extraterrestrial life
**	Human mutation
**	Worldwide epidemic
**	Time travel invented

Self-driving car of the future

Index

A B C

Acknowledgements

Dorling Kindersley would like to thank:
Professor Kevin Warwick, Michael Hilton, Darren Wenn, and Dr David Keating of the Department of Cybernetics, University of Reading (pp. 44–47); Alistair Florence, Carol Highmoor, Paul Fleming and Darren Cockle of Lotus Cars (pp. 54–55); Gary Dalton, Andrew Gower, Paul Murray of BT Laboratories; Tom Fuke of SiliconGraphics Computer Systems, Reading, CADCentre, Cambridge (pp. 48–49); Nicholas C Thompson, Cole Thompson Associates, Architects, Project Director INTEGER Intelligent & Green Housing Project (pp. 20–21); Brian Bloor, Ian Holden, and Tony Davison of IBM United Kingdom Limited; Neil Johannessen, curator of the British Telecom Museum, London; Veneta Paul of the Science Museum, London; Rosie Hayes of the Oxford Institute of Virology and Environmental Biology; Nathan Powell of the Meteorological Office; Millennium Tower Architectural Model (pp. 22–23) designed by Foster Partners for the Obayashi Corporation; SegaWorld; Gerald Armin; Gary Ombler.
Editorial and research assistance: Katie Martin, Joanne Matthews, and Robert Graham
Design assistance: Catharine Goldsmith
Special photography: Steve Gorton, Dave King
Additional photography: Jane Burton, Andy Crawford, Philip Dowell, Philip Garward, Dave King, Ian O'Leary, Tim Ridley, Jane Stockman, Clive Streeter
Illustrators: Joanne Connor, Nicholas Hill
Index: Marion Dent

The publisher would like the following for their kind permission to reproduce their photographs:
(a=above, b=below, c=centre, l=left, r=right; t=top)
AKG, London: Archaeological Museum, Florence 36tr; Arcaid: Neil Troiano 22–23c; Associated Press:

Technos Japan 33c; Chas. A. Blatchford & Sons Ltd: 41bra; Blaupunkt: 25c; Bridgeman Art Library, London/New York: Staatliche Museen, Berlin 8bc; ©British Library Board: 49cr; Reproduced with permission of Applied Research and Technology Department, BT Labs: 4tc, tr, 6tl, bl, 28–29, 59tr, br; The image is reproduced with kind permission from The Coca-Cola Company: 17c; Corbis: Roger Ressmeyer 11tc, 49tr, Michael S. Yamashita 27ca; Corbis-Bettmann: 8tl, 12tl, 34cl; Corbis-Bettmann/UPI: 48tl, 52cla; Daimler Benz: 4bl, 26cl, b; Diners' Club: 10tc; Energy Research and Generation, Inc: 55tr; Ecoscene: John Farhar 12cr; ESA: 59bl; Mary Evans Picture Library: 8cb, cra, 22bl, 26tl, 42bl, 45cl, 57br, 59cla, Sigmund Freud Copyrights 32tr; Future Systems, London: 4c, 19b; John Frost Newspapers: Evening Standard/Solo: Ken Towner 40tr; Pascal Goetgheluck: 58b; The Ronald Grant Archive: The Fifth Element (1997) Guild 27crb, 1984 (1956) Associated British Pathé 14tr, Star Trek: Next Generation (TV) Paramount Television 40b, 2001, A Space Odyssey (1969) MGM 44tl; Robert Harding Picture Library: Charlie Westerman 55tc; Honda (UK): 18cb; Hulton Getty: 8tr, cr, 9cb, crb, 10tl; The Hutchison Library: Bernard Régent 16–17b, Liba Taylor 17tl; The Image Bank/Archive Photos: 58c, Scott Sutton 48cl; Ann Ronan at Image Select: 32tl; IBM: 11tr, 58cl; Courtesy of the Kobal Collection: Robocop Orion Pictures (1987) 40cr; Lotus Cars: 54b; The Met. Office: 15tr; The Movie Store Collection: Batman Forever Warner Bros. (1995) 33tr, The Time Machine MGM/Galaxy (1960) 57tl; NASA: 10cr, 38tl, 50cb, 57tr; National Motor Museum, Beaulieu: 19tl; Natural History Photographic Agency: GI

Bernard 36-37b, Daniel Heuclin 36cr; The Robert Opie Collection: 9tc; Picture courtesy of Panasonic: 53tl; Pepsi IMAX Theatre: 49tl; 'Vision of the future' images supplied by Philips Electronics: 30cl, bl, c, bc, br, 31, 59tl; Psion Computers plc: (screen) 52bc; Quadrant Picture Library: Flight/Wagner 27cl; Rex Features: 10clb, 18cr, 24bl, tl, 26cr, 27bl, 42br, 43br, 55cl, Neil Stevenson 11crb, Greg Williams 13c, ca, 41br; Roslin Institute, Roslin: 37ca; Science Photo Library: 37br, Julian Baum 38cl, 56cl, 57cr, John Bavosi 34tr, A Barrington Brown 10cb, J Bernholc et al North Carolina State University 5c, 54tl, Dale Boyer 12bl, Jean-Loup Charmet 8bl, Custom Medical Stock Photo 34bc, Earth Satellite Corporation 15tl, ESA/PLI 12-13b, Ken Eward 35tl, Simon Fraser 37cr, Simon Fraser/RVI Newcastle-upon-Tyne 36cb, GE Astro Space 12cr, Guntram Gerst, Peter Arnold Inc 12br, GJLP-CNRI 33br, Klaus Guldbrandsen 40bra, 49br, Victor Habbick Visions 56-57c, David Hall 18cl, David Hardy 56bl,W Haxby, Lamont Doherty Earth Obsersavatory 51tr, James Holmes 32-33b, Ducros Jerrican 13bl, 25cl, Mura Jerrican 43bl, James King-Holmes 41tr, 53cb, Mehau Kulyk 34cr, br, Lawrence Livermore National Laboratory: 55b, Massonnet et al/CNES 51tl, John Mead 18bl, Peter Menzel 43cl, Hank Morgan 33tc, 44cb, 45tl, 47cl, c, Nelson Morris 52tl, NASA 11cra, 14bl, 27t, tl, 43tl, NASA Goddard Institute for Space Studies 15cra, NASA/Space Telescope Science Institute 50bl, NCSA/University of Illinois 12cl, NOAA 15tc, David Parker 58cr, Philippe Plailly 32bl, Philippe Plailly/Eurelios 37cr, Catherine Pouedras/MNHN/Eurelios 40c, Rosenfeld Images Ltd 37cr, Volker Steger, Peter Arnold Inc. 40tl, James Stevenson 41tc, Weiss, Jerrican

13tr, US Department of Energy 42l, Erik Viktor 35cl; Science Museum, London: 9cr; Science Museum/Science & Society Picture Library: 4-5b, 6r, 19tc, tr, 22-23t, 41l, 52b, 53c, tr, bc, 54cl, cra, 54-55t; Shimuzu Corporation, Space Systems Division, Tokyo: 22bl; Frank Spooner Pictures: Gamma: Nicolas Le Corre 50br, 51bl, Alexis Duclos 16cl, Kaku Kurita 23b, 43tc, tr, Pascal Maitre 17tr, Gamma Liaison: Steven Burr Williams/simulation display courtesy of Massachusetts Institute of Technology/digital composition by Slim Films 25b; Tony Stone Images: Paul Chesley 22br, 25c, Ross Harrison Koty 51c, Don Lowe 17cl, Andy Sacks 38bl; Sygma: AH Bingen 51br, Hank Morgan 44cb, 45tl, A Nogues 16tl, Ilkka Uimonen 44cb, I Wyman 3clb; Tate Gallery Publications: The Reckless Sleeper (1927) Rene Magritte ©ADAGP, Paris and DACS, London 1998 32c; Telegraph Colour Library: 16cr, 22bc, 25tr, 34bl, 58tr, Paul Windsor 55cr; Vintage Magazine Company: 13tl, 18tl, 24tl, cl, 30tl, 50tl, 50tl, 58tl; Volvo Car Corporation: 50c, cr.
Jacket:
Reproduced with permission of Applied Research and Technology Department, BT Labs: front tl, cra, back tl, cra, clb; Daimler Benz: front tcr, back tcr; Energy Research and Generation, Inc: back cla; Mary Evans Picture Library: back crb, Future Systems, London: front br; 'Vision of the future' images supplied by Philips Electronics: front tc, back tc; Rex Features: back cr; Science Photo Library: Julian Baum front cla, J Bernholc et al North Carolina State University front tr, back tr, spine, Ken Eward front bl, GJLP-CNRI front clb, Lawrence Livermore National Laboratory: back bl, John Mead back br, Peter Menzel back cb; Science Museum / Science & Society Picture Library: inside front r; Frank Spooner Pictures: Gamma: Kaku Kurita inside back tl.